The Tree Whisperer's
10
Tree and Plant
Insights

Jim Conroy, PhD, The Tree Whisperer®
and
Ms. Basia Alexander, Chief Listener

Plant Kingdom
Communications®
PlantKingdomCommunications.com

For Nature Lovers
For the Plant Kingdom
For All of Nature
For the Future

First published in 2013 by Plant Kingdom Communications, Publisher.
P.O. Box 90, Morris Plains, NJ 07950 www.plantkingdomCommunications.com

The mission of Plant Kingdom Communications is
Peace and Dynamic Balance Among the Beings of Earth.

ISBN-13: 978-0-9834114-8-2   ISBN-10: 0-9834114-8-4
Library of Congress Control Number: 2013931524

Plant Kingdom Communications books may be purchased for educational, business, or sales promotional use. For information, please write: Special Markets Department, Plant Kingdom Communications, LLC, P.O. Box 90, Morris Plains, NJ 07950 USA.

The Plant Kingdom Communications Speaker's Bureau can bring authors to your live event. For more information, please go to *www.plantkingdomCommunications.com/Speakers-Bureau*

Printed by Thomson-Shore (www.Thomson-Shore.com) in the United States of America on recycled paper.

Front cover photo of Copper Beech ©Basia Alexander. Thanks to Sheila Labrecque for her lovely Copper Beech tree and for being a real Tree Protector.

Back cover photo by ©Jane B. Kellner, Kelley/Kellner Associates, Salisbury, CT

Cover design by Basia Alexander and Jim Conroy. Interior design by Basia Alexander.

IMPORTANT NOTES FOR THE READER: The material in this book is intended to provide an overview of the research and techniques of Tree Whispering. This material is referenced at CooperativeBioBalance.org for the reader who wishes to pursue further inquiries and study. Undertaking any of this book's suggestions for techniques, treatments, or lifestyle changes referred to or implied in this book are the reader's responsibility. The ideas, suggestions, and techniques presented for use in this book should not be used in place of qualified medical/professional advice. This book is sold with the understanding that the publisher and/or authors are not engaged in rendering psychological services, and are in no way liable for use or misuse of the ideas, suggestions, and/or techniques.

While the authors have made every effort to provide accurate Internet addresses at the time of publication, neither the publisher nor the authors assume any responsibility for errors, or for changes that occur after publication. Further, the publisher does not have any control over and does not assume any responsibility for author or third-party websites or their content.

 Table Of Contents

When we try to pick out anything by itself, we find it hitched to everything else in the universe.

JOHN MUIR
AMERICAN NATURALIST, EXPLORER, AND WRITER, 1838–1914

We cannot solve our problems with the same thinking we used when we created those problems.

ATTRIBUTED TO ALBERT EINSTEIN
GERMAN-AMERICAN PHYSICIST, 1879–1955

A tree is beautiful, but what's more, it has a right to life; like water, the sun and the stars, it is essential. Life on earth is inconceivable without trees. Forests create climate, climate influences peoples' character, and so on and so forth.

ANTON PAVLOVICH CHEKHOV
RUSSIAN AUTHOR, DRAMATIST, AND PHYSICIAN, 1860–1904

Trees are the earth's endless effort to speak to the listening heaven.

RABINDRANATH TAGOR
BENGALI NOBEL PRIZE WINNING AUTHOR, 1861–1941

Where the Insights Come From

Dr. Jim Conroy, The Tree Whisperer®, remembers: I do my research and development on annuals and crops at an organic community-supported garden in northern New Jersey. One year, the Davis variety green bean seedlings grew as far as their second bract of leaves when there was a cold snap—no sun, lots of rain—that lasted over two weeks. The small seedlings had a problem: Should they let their roots drown? Or, should they let their stem and leaf tissues become waterlogged? With so little sunlight for transpiration and photosynthesis, do they pull as much water as they can up from their roots taking the risk of imbalancing the water, sugar, and nutrient ratio in their tissues? Or, do they let some precious roots drown?

This was a life-and-death dilemma for the little bean plants.

And, it taught me great lessons. Whether large or small, old or young, it is true that trees and plants are alive. They face challenges just as people do, and they deserve our respect.

I was able to help the green bean plants bring their inner physiologies into a more balanced inner state. The seedlings were able to hold themselves in that balanced state for a few days so that they could tolerate the extreme environmental factors. Then the rain stopped and the sun came out. They went on to grow into healthy and productive mature bean plants.

Dr. Jim talks about trees: People think that just because it rains after a drought, a tree begins to drink the water and is over the drought stress. Usually, the tree is more like a sailor on the ocean, saying "water, water, everywhere and not a drop to drink." Why? Many trees lose their ability to take up water after they have been drought-stressed. It's easy to see that stress would compromise the internal functionality of the tree. An example for people might be prolonged lack of sleep. One good night's sleep helps, but it does not return the body to full health. Sleep deprivation may have taken a toll which people don't get over easily.

When it is stressed, a tree cannot easily repair or restore its own health. For example, its fluid transportation system may have slowed and there may be blockages in various places. This is sometimes why you will see sap oozing out of the lower trunk of a tree.

Here's another example of why a tree cannot restore its own health easily. Some of a tree's cells—such as the cells in the growing zones—may have lost the ability to divide. That's why you might see small leaf buds in autumn, or very few leaf buds at all. This is dangerous for the tree because it will need new leaves in order to produce food for itself in the next season.

Dr. Jim recommends asking the trees: How do I know these things? It's true that I have the scientific background to do a visual or external evaluation because I earned my doctorate degree in Plant Pathology from a prestigious university and spent over 25 years working as a top executive in plant health-related corporations. But, I actually know how trees and plants operate on the inside because I ask them.

I believe—and science is now showing—that Green Beings have a unique kind of cognition: they can do cost/benefit analysis, recognize self from non-self, and other amazing feats.[1]

I know there is a deep intelligence within Nature that people can communicate with. The communication begins when a person's Life Force or bioenergy field overlaps with the bioenergy field of a tree or plant just by being close or touching it.[2 & 3] Then, the person becomes quiet inside, feels heart-based caring, and allows intuition to receive information.

I call it "getting in touch with the Growth Energy" of trees and plants. Anyone can do it.

When I touch a tree, sure, I feel the bark, but I also feel the tree's Life Force flowing through it. I feel a flow of power, like a current, moving from the roots to the branches and leaves. This force tells me a mosaic of details about the tree's whole and interacting inner health in ways that conventional science and technology cannot define.

The first step for me is to bond with the Life Force and biofield of the tree or plant.[4] I get into *the zone* by allowing myself to relax into the sensations of being near the tree. My hands feel like they are slipping inside of gloves as I touch the tree's bioenergy field. I feel its unique bioenergy signature inside my heart or in my gut. Sometimes I can hear words or listen to the tree's song. I often smell its fragrance directly from the trunk. I sink into a deep meditative state even though my eyes may still be open.

Let me pause to point out that this is a sacred experience for me. Being with a tree in such an intimate—even spiritual—way is often too great for words. Yet, I want you to have an idea of what it is like for me.

So, when I say that I ask trees and plants about their health, that's just what I do. By touching them, opening my intuition, and using my system, I ask questions and get answers. The trees and plants talk to me that way. I discover malfunctions within their inner physiology. Then, I holistically restore their health using my proprietary bioenergy healing techniques.

Dr. Jim talks about his healing approach: Why am I called The Tree Whisperer®? When I lean close and put my hands on the trunk of a tree in order to feel its Life Force, I suppose it looks like I am whispering with it. But, I don't have a casual conversation. I am dedicated to restoring inner functionality and rejuvenating the health of trees, plants, and entire ecosystems.

I use hands-on, energy-healing methods similar to those now commonly accepted in hospitals. Energy-medicine techniques now proven effective for people include Reiki, Polarity, Touch-for-Health, Healing Touch, the BodyTalk System, Matrix Energetics, and more.

My bioenergy-healing methods are for trees and plants, as well for as small and large ecosystems. The systems I created are called Tree Whispering®, the Green Centrics™ System, Co-Existence Technologies™, and Cooperative BioBalance®.5

There are no products whatsoever involved in my bioenergy healing. After a tree's or plant's health is rejuvenated, only then do products become usable *for the tree*. If circulation is blocked, *from the tree's point of view*, all the fertilizer in the world won't help it. I always say, "Get the tree healthy on the inside *first*, then use products to *keep* the tree healthy."

The Tree Whisperer gives some history: In 2002, I started creating the Green Centrics™ System as an organized, professional, proprietary methodology. In early days of developing the system, trees and plants taught me why stress factors are additive for them and that three or more stresses can lead to their decline. After three years of research and development, I started doing this methodology professionally. My customers started calling me their "tree whisperer."

My business partner, Basia Alexander, suggested that we go to public appearances and professional trade shows with a sign that said "The Tree Whisperer." Initially, I went with some hesitation. But, people's reactions showed that they understood. I embraced the moniker. The name The Tree Whisperer® expresses what I do in a way that most people can grasp quickly and with a smile.

Not long afterward, I realized that people want a simple and easy way to help their own trees and to feel a deeper appreciation for all of Nature. So, Basia and I created Tree Whispering® and started teaching classes to eager tree and plant lovers.

Dr. Jim elaborates: To fully understand Tree Whispering, a shift in thinking is needed. People are accustomed to assuming that they know what is best for trees, but, in truth, they should ask trees about the trees' inner health and about how to work with trees in partnership.

You might be thinking: "Is he crazy? He's saying that I should ask a tree!" No. I am not crazy. Both wilderness trackers as well as indigenous peoples have always known how to pay close attention to Nature. They pay attention to physical signs like changes in foliage or animal footprints, but—more importantly— they pay attention to their gut feelings and intuitions. We Westerners—who believe we are so advanced—need to transform our mindset. It is crazy *not* to listen closely to Nature. Our enjoyment of a walk in the woods—if not our very lives and our future on the planet—may depend on cultivating such listening skills.

Ms. Basia Alexander, Chief Listener, explains how: My personal best sensitivity is that of listening to the intelligence within Nature. I'm called the Chief Listener because of the early days of developing the systems. Dr. Jim would return to the office with more questions than answers. He would describe what he felt and saw. I would listen. It was in the quiet of my listening that Dr. Jim could re-create his experience with the plant or tree in order to have insights into what was happening inside of it. By asking questions and listening, I helped him build the processes by which he would heal trees and plants.

Every person has a best sense: sight, hearing, touch, smell, or taste. You can find yours and then expand it. Tree Whispering can begin for you as a personal sensory experience of the Growth Energy and Life Force of trees or plants in a simple way.

I recommend that you go outside with great curiosity and open-mindedness. You may go into your backyard, or walk through a park or forest. You may sit down quietly. Don't have great expectations, but do expect to have a good time. Just tell yourself that you can connect with the living Being that is a tree or plant. Allow yourself to use all your senses, gut feelings, or intuition.

Expressing gratitude quietly in your heart is the best way to start. Then, sit quietly and receive sensations, images, sounds, thoughts, feelings, impressions, fragrances, insights, or pleasure. If the experience is not pleasant, then stop.

Take whatever you get. Don't invalidate any thought. It's not just coming from you! Information is coming *to* you from Nature *through* thoughts. Permit thoughts to come. Write them down.

Accept your feelings. Emotional awareness is often a good way to open the door. Allow yourself to be peaceful and trusting. Know that you are connecting and communicating with Nature—with another form of life on this beautiful planet. It is an adventure, if you'll only let it happen and trust it.

> **Have A Personal Experience of Communication with a Tree or Plant**
>
> 1. Have curiosity and open-mindedness.
> 2. Walk outside where trees and plants are.
> 3. Expect to have a good time.
> 4. Tell yourself you can connect or communicate with another living Being.
> 5. Allow yourself to use all your senses, gut feelings, or intuition while relaxing.
> 6. Begin by quietly expressing gratitude.
> 7. Sit quietly and receive sensations, images, sounds, thoughts, feelings, impressions, fragrances, insights, or pleasure. If the experience is not pleasant, then stop.
> 8. Permit all thoughts. Accept all feelings. If you want to, write them down.
> 9. Enjoy the adventure of stepping inside the world of another living Being.

Realize that your experience will be unique to you. You may believe that you have received a message. Enjoy it! You may want to whisper a message back to the Green Being. Go ahead and do that! Or, if you feel peaceful and calm, that may be Nature's peace and calm resonating inside of you.

Basia describes teaching: The first thing we do is tell people that *coming from the tree's point of view* is possible. We think that having a more enlightened kind of relationship with trees, plants, and all of Nature can enhance the quality of people's lives. Students see how taking respectful actions toward all plants is good for themselves and sustainable for the planet.

Then, you may want to go further. You may want to learn the simple and easy techniques of Tree Whispering®. You'll be helping trees and plants that are sick or stressed. You can learn in our classes or workshops in just hours! The exercises and methods I have mentioned are available in more detail in our two books, *Tree Whispering: A Nature Lover's Guide to Touching, Healing, and Communicating with Trees, Plants, and All of Nature* and *Tree Whispering: Trust the Path Notebook and Journal.*

Some people think that our techniques will help them make the plant grow a certain way, make the crop yield more, or make the tree do what they want it to do. That is not true! Usually, those people cannot let go of their desire to dominate Nature. We believe in partnership and cooperation with Nature. We caution students against any attempts to control or manipulate trees and plants. Control and manipulation never works anyway, in the long run. It always backfires on people because of the way that it throws living systems out of balance.

Dr. Jim describes what he does: When I treat, I am getting to know a tree or plant as an individual. I am coming from its point of view. Mostly, I am asking it about what conditions must be corrected in its internal functionality in order to improve its health. Yes, they contain that information since they are living systems, but they can't always accomplish the change in internal functionality for themselves. It's just like us. We might know about our own illnesses, but we can't always heal ourselves.

I don't use products or invasive techniques. I heal in these ways: by establishing a personal rapport—like being *in the zone*—with the tree's Life Force, by focusing my conscious intentionality, and by moving bioenergy flows within and around the tree. Trees may be different than people, but since they are alive, they respond to bioenergy medicine healing techniques, too.

Dr. Jim reveals what he has learned: For years, I have been listening to trees and plants, learning how to come from their points of view. To do that, I have had to set aside my own personal point of view. I have learned to ask the plants and trees what is best for them and to have humility in doing so.

I have also had to come to terms with my investments in advanced education and a corporate career. My formal training consisted of indoctrination in the scientific mindset and instruction in methodologies for controlling and manipulating plants. In developing Tree Whispering® and Green Centrics™, I let go of my human-centric agenda. I had to liberate myself from my training. What I thought was right turned out to be often wrongly used. What I was taught should be done to trees and plants may not have been in their best interests. I did a full turn-around; I left the corporate world and struck out to do what I felt and still feel is a higher calling.

Dr. Jim explains his insights: In all the years I have touched and communicated with trees and plants, I have accumulated a lot of practical knowledge of their secret ways. I have come to trust the consistency of my experience. Intuition plays a role in generating these insights. Intuition uses the right-brain functions of nonlinearity and wholeness. So, I feel that my intuition is a powerful ally. And, you might say that my working conditions are conducive to spiritual kinds of experiences. Standing quietly with my hands on a tree's trunk and feeling its biofield, is a meditative and revelatory experience. So, I come to know about trees' and plants' lives directly from their Source.

Trees and plants have shared much with me about their inner physical workings as well as their more mysterious ways. Knowing about their workings through the insights of this book will help you expand your relationship with them and will provide guidance in your healing efforts with them.

The discoveries I have made depart from the conventional, linear-thinking interpretation of trees and plants as mechanisms. My insights are discoveries that come through valid ways of knowing that complement modern scientific method.

Basia adds something about ways of knowing: Dr. Edmund Bourne's book *Global Shift—How a New Worldview is Transforming Humanity* details the coming expansion of people's attitudes. He says that the ancient and indigenous ways of knowing the world through experience, empathy, intuition, or even mystical perceptions suffered near extinction as a result of the rise of the scientific method over the last 400 years or so. Now, he says, those ways of knowing are on the comeback. *6*

Dr. Jim and I believe that our work is on the leading edge in the new, burgeoning field of what Bourne calls "participatory and subjective" methodologies for acquiring valid knowledge. We strongly believe that personal engagement and experience with a life form such as a tree or plant both supplements and reinforces objective, repeatable science.

Dr. Jim emphasizes: I believe that all of us, as the human guardians of Earth, can cooperate to bring ecosystems and the living Beings of Nature back into dynamic balance. Trees, plants, insects, diseases—even entire ecosystems—can again work in harmony and dynamic balance. I believe that balance can be reestablished in Nature, but *not* because we are so smart, *not* because our science has all the answers, *not* because we can control or manipulate Nature. We can't control Nature. Attempts to dominate Nature have not worked out well.

Instead, reestablishment of harmony and balance can result from our conscious and co-creative partnership with Nature. I call this new kind of relationship with Nature "Cooperative BioBalance."

Through the practice of Tree Whispering, you can establish a personal partnership with your own trees and plants. You can help them thrive and grow with a holistic, respectful, bioenergy-based healing approach, and it's good for your well-being, too.

My ten tree and plant insights are the result of years of talking with trees, plants, and also other ecosystem members. I am grateful that they have given me the gifts of their experience and wisdom about living on this planet for millenia. Their lives are precious to me.

Basia and I are thankful that you want to learn their insights, too.

Insight 1:
Healthy-Looking Trees May Not Be Healthy On The Inside and Must Manage Their Inner Resources

THE 12 TREE AND PLANT STRESS FACTORS

Dr. Jim Conroy, The Tree Whisperer®, says: The story I told at the beginning of the previous chapter—about the Davis variety green beans and their life-or-death dilemma—shows how complex and sophisticated a plant's inner functionality truely is. Modern scientific research is starting to understand that plants are sensitive organisms that have an internal and external information network structure.

> *...Plants accurately compute inputs from the environment, use sophisticated cost-benefit analysis, and take action to mitigate diverse environmental insults.*
>
> *Plants are also capable of refined recognition of self and non-self, ... This view sees plants as information processing organisms with complex, long-distance communication systems within the plant body and extending into the surrounding ecosystem...*[1]

FROM THE MISSION STATEMENT OF THE
SOCIETY FOR PLANT SIGNALING AND BEHAVIOR
WWW.PLANTBEHAVIOR.ORG/ABOUT

These scientific conclusions correspond to my first insight: *Healthy-looking trees and plants may not be healthy on the inside and must manage their inner resources.*

I tell people, "Do the right things from the beginning to keep your trees and plants healthy." Despite people's best efforts, trees and plants still can get stressed. With current weather extremes, most trees are stressed to some degree.

12 Tree and Plant Stress Factors

1. Current conditions: too hot, too cold, too wet, too dry, poor lighting, flooding, standing water, drought, etc., or some combination of the above.

2. Multiple-season and multiple-year stress factors that are additive: ie. summer drought followed by extremely cold winter and/or a cold and wet spring followed by extreme heat. Other additive factors include lightning hits, splitting, etc.

3. Human factors: ie. root loss in transplanting, originally planted too deep, "volcano" mulch piles, piling soil at base, digging around base, construction, changes in land grade or topography, improper pruning, bands or ties left on trunk, compacted soil, removing autumn leaves, hit by car, abuses like carving, "topping," road salt, etc.

4. Poor soil composition, fertility, or drainage.

5. Competition from unwanted plants, often called "weeds."

6. Animal damage: chewing, digging, rubbing, eating, tunneling, urinating, climbing, etc.

7. Excess or inappropriate use of any product (such as harsh fertilizers or protective sprays) or invasive techniques (such as air spading, harsh pruning).

8. Pollution of soil, air, and/or water.

9. Global or local environmental or climate changes: different rainfall amounts, change in season length, survival of insects/diseases, composition of local ecosystem (invasive or nonnative plants, diseases, or insects), different average temperatures or higher night-time temperatures, change in level of water table, excess sun intensity, etc.

10. Any combinations of the above nine factors.

11. Biotic stress factors: direct interactions with harmful insects and diseases—which usually come after other stress factors— weaken the tree's or plant's inner functions.

12. Vicious cycle: uncorrected inner functionality or physiological imbalance(s) open the door to more additive dysfunctions inside the tree or plant, then more insects and diseases are attracted, often leading to decline.

Dr. Jim asks: Which comes first—insects and diseases or weakness in the tree's health? I say that it is weakness in the tree's inner health that generally calls forth insects and diseases. When a tree is sick, it sends out signals that attract them.

Many people think that diseases and insects cause weakness in trees and plants. They do, but it is additive. That is, the internal workings of the tree or plant were initially weak, which attracted the insects or diseases. Just like you and me, if we are run down, then we are more susceptible to catching a cold.

Many companies promote the idea that so-called "bad guys" —insects, diseases, and unwanted plants—attack otherwise healthy trees or plants. Except for very aggressive and sometimes nonlocal insects and diseases, it is the weakness in the tree's health that comes first.

What are the stress factors that weaken a tree's or plant's health and deplete its vitality? See the list on the left.

Extremes in the environment are the most common stress factors. Here, I mean too hot, too cold, too wet, too dry, or some combination. These are additive over seasons and years. Many people think that when rain finally comes after a hot and dry spell, the trees will absorb water and be healthy. Very healthy trees might do that. However, to a tree that is already stressed, heat and dryness cause additive damage.

Even with the best of intentions, people often do the wrong things. Trees and plants may be planted in poor soil or in the wrong place. People plant too deep or pile mulch too high over roots—cutting off precious air and promoting rotting bacteria. When doing construction around trees, even some professionals will regrade the land, thereby burying the trees under too much soil. More than an inch or two is actually too much. In an attempt to give a transplanted tree bracing, bands and ties might be left on too long. These will choke a tree's flow of fluids.

A tree is alive. Just like a person, a tree or plant needs to breathe, to drink water, and to live in a clean, bright place.

HEALTHY-LOOKING TREES MAY NOT BE HEALTHY ON THE INSIDE

Dr. Jim warns: Don't be fooled by trees that are well established or that seem to have lush canopies. They may look good on the outside but aren't always healthy on the inside.

How would you know?

Sometimes there are telltale signs like bleeding canker disease on this pictured Copper Beech tree in Greenwich, Connecticut. This was not surprising because many Beech trees on the East Coast of the United States are weak.

One day, I found the clue—bleeding canker spots—on the Copper Beech that indicated compromised processes inside the tree.

After bioenergy healing treatment, the tree's inner functionality was strengthened and it regained the ability to heal itself. The bleeding canker cleared.

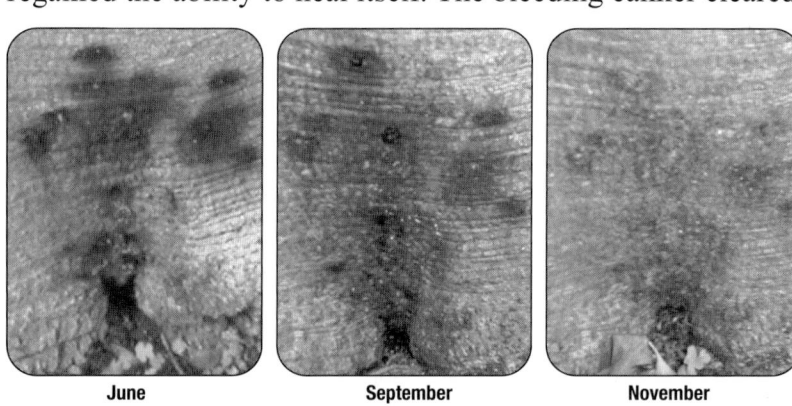

| June | September | November |

I described my general approach to hands-on healing on pages 2–3 and 6–7 of this book.

If you are curious, detailed descriptions of my tree and plant healing techniques are available in Chapters 6 and 7 of Basia's and my book *Tree Whispering: A Nature Lover's Guide to Touching, Healing, and Communicating with Trees, Plants, and All of Nature.*

While some species have their particular telltale signs of inner weakness, such as bleeding cankers, many others do not. It can be a real problem in observing a tree's health.

How would you know if a tree looks healthy on the outside but is really sick on the inside? The best way is to *ask* the tree's innate intelligence about its health and listen or *perceive* carefully for its answer.

Ms. Basia Alexander, Chief Listener, advises: Plants and trees don't have mouths, but we know that they have a lot to say to us. Trees and plants are doing something akin to broadcasting resonance waves or signals because they are alive. It is up to us to expand our skills of receptivity and perception to get their nonverbal communications.

Insects have evolved acute abilities to receive information from plants. We didn't evolve insect eyes or antenna, but we did evolve with sensitive nervous and electrical systems. Sadly, modern city lifestyles and the Western mindset of intellectual orientation have robbed us of the acutely developed sensitivities that our ancestors must have had in order to live, survive, and thrive in their wild natural environment. But, we can redevelop those sensitivities and skills.

> **How to Receive Nonverbal Information**
> * *Through heightened awareness of and the use of any or all of the five physical senses*
> * *Through uninhibited emotional engagement*
> * *Using intuitive perception: a blend of left-brain logic, right-brain creativity, and heart-oriented inspiration*
>   * *Inner seeing...the "mind's eye"*
>   * *Inner hearing...the "little voice inside"*
>   * *Inner knowing...comprehending the heart's truth. This doesn't necessarily need logic or linear thinking.*
> * *By asking "yes" and "no" questions while the nervous and electrical systems are in a bioenergy overlap with another living system...and allowing the answers to come*

How do you do expand your sensitivities?

Be trusting and allowing. Maybe you are a bit analytical—not getting into the fun of it. Just remember that connecting and communicating with another living Being is an adventure. You are stepping into a new world and can bring back a great story to tell. Above all, have a good time!

Are you skeptical? That's okay. There is a place for doubt and questioning as long as you don't close your heart to possibilities.

MANAGING THEIR RESOURCES: BECOMING MORE EFFICIENT

Dr. Jim and the Birch Trees in Randolph, New Jersey:
In 2011, there was a severe late October snow storm on the East Coast of the USA. People called it the Halloween Storm, and it was scary. Trees were still wearing most of their leaves at the time the storm hit, so countless limbs were lost. A homeowner called the following April with concerns about a clump of River Birches. Their tops snapped off. They lost many side limbs, too.

When I connected with the Birch trees, they told me that the branches they lost were important to their food production capacity. It's important to remember that trees and plants make their own food in their leaves. Unlike plants, we can't make our own food inside of our bodies. The Birch trees, as all trees, were aimed toward new growth. The loss of so much leaf-surface meant they would have less energy available.

I come from the tree's point of view and they tell me their ways. So here is generally how seasonal growth works for many trees in temperate climates, as the trees see it.

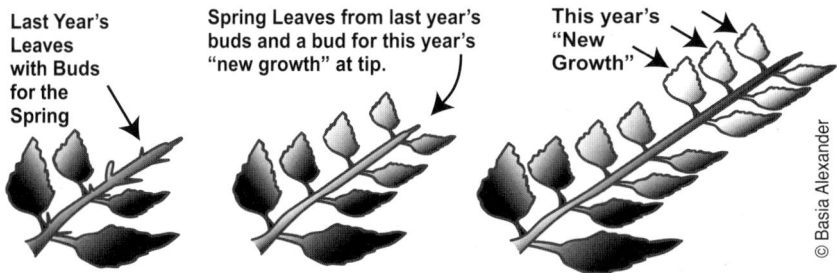

In late summer, trees send energy from the year's food production to the base of existing leaves and to the ends of their branches to make leaf-buds. Those buds are kept alive even as the tree goes into low activity during the cold of winter. In spring, the tree activates its food reserves—kept mostly in the roots—and pushes that food-energy up so that the buds will burst forth as leaves. Those new leaves may *not* be considered new growth for the tree. *They are the gift from last year's growth.*

If the tree is healthy, it will use the food made in those spring leaves to make many new branches and leaves for this new year. The more new growth the tree can make means more food for itself. More food means more growth, thus the cycle continues, and the better off it is.

The tree does a similar thing with growing *new roots* and growing new cells *around its girth* since they support overall growth. Thus overall growth in size is a combination of inter-connected growth-factors in leaves, branches, roots, and girth. Growth is a tree's purpose. Everything it does is aimed toward supporting more growth everywhere in its physical structure.

As a part of sustaining themselves, the Birch trees had enough energy to push out leaves from the previous year's buds that they still had on existing branches. But, to continue a growth cycle with new leaves in the current year, they needed more food-energy. In other words, last year's buds would give them enough leaves to keep them alive but it would not be enough to let them produce and support new leaves this year. They needed the food that would have come from that lost leaf surface-area to put on the new growth this season.

How would they be able to keep themselves going?

RIVER BIRCHES IN RANDOLPH, NJ: We need to produce enough food to sustain ourselves and put on new growth. This involves overlapping of photosynthesis, overall functionality, and growth.

If our systems are efficient, we need less food-energy to sustain ourselves and thus more is available to put on new growth this season. This is important since we lost limbs, and therefore buds, last fall. Since we lost potential leaves, we lost some food-making capacity that would help us make new growth.

New growth means more leaves which means more food which means more growth. Then the cycle can continue.

Our purpose in general is growth. We are always moving towards growth. Everything we do backs up into achieving growth. If we are always moving towards growth, we can ask you, "How do we get there given that we lost branches and buds?"

Help us make our processes more efficient. With more efficient inner processes, that means less energy needed to sustain ourselves and more energy available for our purpose, which is to grow. More energy available means more new growth and more health for us. Less energy available means less new growth.

Once we start growing then we can continue that cycle of more leaves, more food, more growth.

Dr. Jim continues: Though my permission-based, hands-on treatment, I opened my heart to overlap my bioenergy field with the trees' biofield. Then, I used consciously focused energy-healing methodologies with the Birches' internal processes so that their inner functionality would become more efficient.

The trees told me where their energy roadblocks were. My interactions with the trees' bioenergy fields cleared those blockages.

Generally speaking, the trees guided me to get their overlapping network patterns of photosynthesis, functionality including circulation, and cellular growth processes all interacting properly and working in proper synchronization.

Thus, the trees' internal processes became more energy-efficient and they were able to move more energy towards their purpose: producing this year's growth.

The photo on the left was taken in autumn of 2012, almost a year to the day after the Halloween Storm. With most leaves already dropped, it's easy to see how many new branches the Birches added this year where their tops were snapped off. A less efficient tree would not have been able to produce this much new growth.

MANAGING THEIR RESOURCES: AN ALL-OR-NOTHING BID

Dr. Jim tells the Greenwich, Connecticut, Hickory story:
It was late August in Connecticut and my client's Hickory tree had very few leaves on it, and those leaves were small. It was probably suffering from two major stress factors but was not quite in decline. However, it was a likely candidate for decline because it could not produce much food with few, small leaves.

The Hickory's healing session consisted of a patchwork of network patterns cobbled together which I didn't understand at the time. This might sound mysterious or cryptic, but I'll briefly relay the topics from my treatment notes:

• *Getting growth processes moving*

• *Maximizing photosynthesis*

• *Maximizing the uptake of water and nutrients.*

• *Once those processes were in place, the tree wanted the trio of functionality/new growth/new leaves to be connected with the definition: "health, food production, and new growth."*

• *The last connection established dynamic balance within the tree as "repair/health/new growth" with "filling out" and "being beautiful."*

I didn't understand the combination at the time, but I accepted that the tree's innate intelligence knew what it wanted so I left it at that. I trusted the path upon which I was being guided by Nature's consciousness.

At the end of the session, the Hickory told me: **"Now, I will heal."**

Normally, I would expect the results of an August healing treatment to show up the following spring. But, two weeks later I saw that the tree put on abundant new leaves. I was shocked!

In that very short span of tree-time and even though it was late in the season, the Hickory used its remaining resources to push out new leaves immediately. By committing all of its resources—in an all-or-nothing bid—it was now able to bring itself back to health, produce more food to survive the winter, and would be able to push out new leaves the next spring.

Hickory Tree: I will use up my energy now to make more food for myself. I will risk this: I will not conserve that energy to try to live through the winter and try to make leaves in spring. I want to get healthy, put on new growth, fill out, and be beautiful.

Dr. Jim recounts: I was concerned about its ability to push out new leaves the next spring since it seemed to have used up its buds. But, leafing out in late summer, made sense in order for it to produce more food and set up its own growing↔healing cycle. It may have conserved a few buds and it was also able to set new buds. Setting new buds means that a plant or tree creates specific new tissues that will become leaves. In a subsequent, short healing session late that Autumn, I helped it to increase its circulation of fluids to the leaf buds, replacing unhealthy cells with healthy cells.

The Hickory had probably undergone more than one stress factor before I originally arrived. Then, my consciously focused, hands-on bioenergy healing treatment gave it the boost it needed to manage its remaining resources and do the right things to heal itself. Sure enough, the next spring it was on-the-spot with abundant, large, new leaves. It grew with lush, beautiful growth and regained its health throughout the rest of that year.

MANAGING THEIR RESOURCES: A LIFE-OR-DEATH DILEMMA

Dr. Jim and the Huntington, West Virginia, golf course tree: As I walked the perimeter of a West Virginia golf course in springtime, checking the trees, I heard a loud and plaintive cry for help in my inner hearing from behind an adjacent house. The tree had no leaves even though surrounding trees were leafing out abundantly. I went over and put my hands on it.

The tree was in a dilemma. It was concerned about using up its remaining resources to push out leaves from its buds for the new season since it did not think it could make more food to sustain itself once it pushed out those leaves. It knew it had only so much food-resources.

GOLF COURSE TREE: If I use that food to push out new leaves, and I can't make more food for myself, then I can't sustain myself. I will die.

The tree was going to just sit there; it wasn't going to use that energy up to push out new leaves since it didn't think it could make more food for itself.

During the intuitive bioenergy overlap of treatment, I discovered a major disconnect between photosynthesis and circulation. The tree already knew about it. Once I understood the tree's dilemma and used my healing techniques to connect photosynthesis and circulation, the tree said this.

GOLF COURSE TREE: I'll push out my leaves now because I know I can make more food for myself and survive.

Dr. Jim continues: I think this shows the deep intelligence within Nature. The tree was aware—on some level—about its dilemma. It didn't know how to get out of it. But, it did know that if it saved its resources by not pushing out leaves, that would give it more time to survive.

Insight 2:
Trees and Plants Don't Recover From Stress Factors Easily Because Stress Compromises Internal Functionality

STRESS IS ADDITIVE

Dr. Jim says: Let's say, in your day-to-day life, you have lots of deadlines at work and spend sleepless nights during that time. Then, an emergency occurs within your family. Sound familiar? If you were healthy, you could probably handle one of the stress conditions at a time without ill effects. But, put one stress on top of another and another, then your health may be compromised.

It's the same with trees. Not only don't they recover from stress factors easily, but, those stresses add up. Take the stress factors listed on page 10 very seriously. Trees may not be as resilient as you think.

Sometimes trees look healthy to a casual observer, but their inner functionality is compromised. Once compromised, they don't get over the effects of multiple stress factors and can go into what I call the "pulling in" pattern of decline.

STRESS COMPROMISES INTERNAL FUNCTIONALITY

Dr. Jim explains: When I describe to people that stress compromises inner functionality, they understand it immediately. It tracks with experiences in their own bodies. Like trees, people are sometimes ill but show no telltale signs.

However, the idea—stress deteriorates the inner functionality of trees and plants—goes generally unrecognized in conventional tree and plant care. Existing professional tools and methods can, at best, measure one or two systems, not a tree's inner operations *as a whole.*

Also there are no products that can repair trees' or plant's inner feedback loops or balance the totality of interrelationships. Products won't ever be able to restore a whole tree to health or its inner functionality to dynamic balance. There are just too many variables involved in healthy dynamic balance. Products can be useful, and I recommend using products to *keep* trees and plants healthy when they are *already* healthy on the inside.

Overall, since there is no cookie-cutter solution, the idea of stress compromising natural functionality is usually ignored.

One of Basia's and my goals is to inspire people to have a new kind of personal experience with Nature. We hope that you will expand your relationship with trees and plants by learning to take their perspective. It is our hope that when you come from their point of view, you may not be so quick to put products on your trees and plants without *asking* them.

Dr. Jim continues: In Insight #1, you read the list of 12 Stress Factors. Let me give you an example of how *multiple* stress factors compromise inner functionality. Let's say there is a sequence of three stress factors: too wet in spring, too hot and dry in summer, and then too cold in winter.

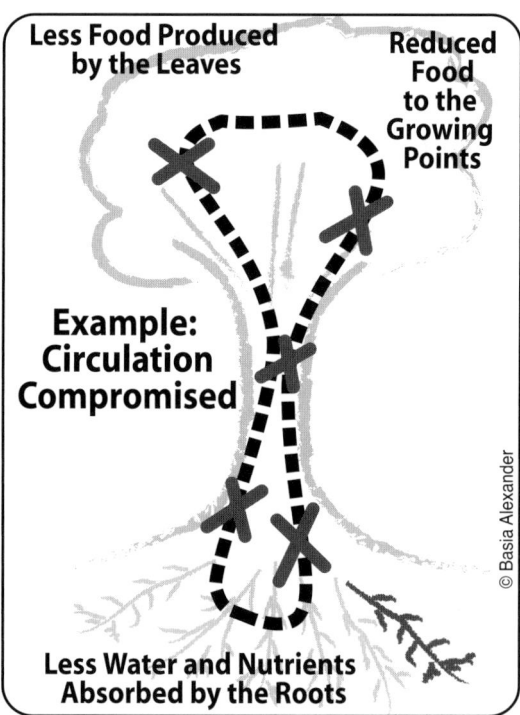

Less Food Produced by the Leaves

Reduced Food to the Growing Points

Example: Circulation Compromised

© Basia Alexander

Less Water and Nutrients Absorbed by the Roots

A tree's circulation will often become compromised in such a situation. This means that less water and nutrients are absorbed by the roots.

So, less water and nutrients flow up to the leaves to be available for photosynthesis. Without the proper amount of water and nutrients, there is less photosynthesis.

Less photosynthesis means less food is produced by the tree for its growth.

Then, *because* circulation is compromised, whatever little food is produced doesn't travel to the growing zones or to the roots for storage.

Overall, less food means less fuel to support the tree's growth. With less food being produced by the tree, and a compromised circulation system, then less food, water, and nutrients are able to get to the growing points, such as leaf buds, girth cells, or roots tips.

Less growth along with continued degradation of circulation and food production then starts a downward spiral toward decline.

Other interior systems will be compromised, too. For instance, there will be an imbalance in the ratio of nutrients, sugars, and water. I call this the "plant chemistry." There will also be reduced or stagnant cell division, which will stunt growth.

Dr. Jim answers a key question: How do trees and plants cope with stress? They have amazing and sophisticated chemical and physiological responses which they muster to cope with both the abiotic (nonliving) and the biotic (living) stress factors.

However, mustering these responses takes a toll. They use precious energy to compensate. Think of how a train dispatcher operates. He or she has trains rolling, trains waiting, and trains needing to cross paths. Also, if one of the switches goes down, trains have to be rerouted. The dispatcher has to prioritize.

Trees cope by rerouting and reprioritizing their dwindling resources. The rerouting itself takes fuel and energy from the tree. Sometimes they will sacrifice an older or an upper branch; they stop sending resources to it so that they can use their declining resources more efficiently on newer or closer-in tissue.

Dr. Jim's perspective from inside: The use of products such as fertilizers, bug killers, or growth regulators has unanticipated negative consequences for trees. If you were standing in their roots, *coming from their point of view,* as I do, you would realize that a sick tree must use part of its precious energy resources to chemically break down those products.

From the tree's or plant's point of view, such products may have some temporary positive effects—such as reducing populations of aggressive insects—but they are not the answer to restoring health. And, very often the insects or diseases rebound with a vengeance because the tree is weaker than it was before. The trees' or plants' inner health needs to be restored.

NETWORK PATTERNS OF INTERACTION

Dr. Jim mentions feedback loops: The illustration of compromised circulation on page 20 shows clearly how trees and plants operate in feedback loops. Every system and function is connected to every other system and function.

Shown in this illustration, each labeled network pattern can refer

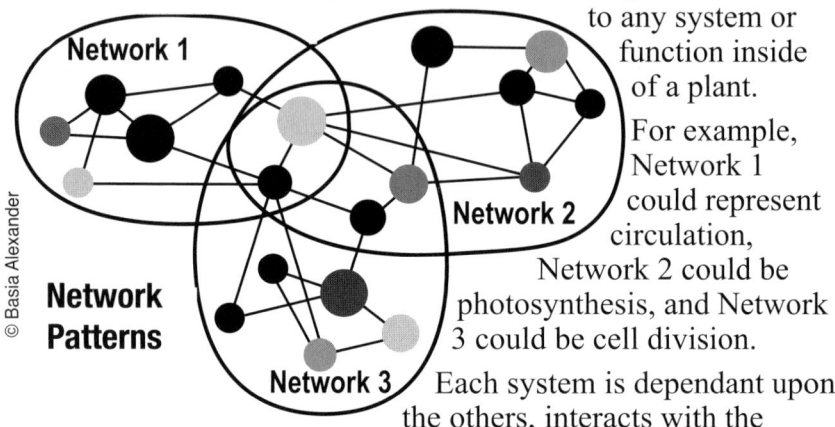

to any system or function inside of a plant. For example, Network 1 could represent circulation, Network 2 could be photosynthesis, and Network 3 could be cell division. Each system is dependant upon the others, interacts with the others, and supports the others. It's a finely tuned orchestra of physical relationships and bioenergy interactions. It is clear that disturbing any single part of these loops, disturbs the whole looping system and therefore compromises inner functionality.

Dr. Jim talks about ecosystems: Additionally, all related organisms such as insects and diseases also operate in interactive feedback loops with trees and plants in ecosystems, too. So you can imagine in the illustration that Network 1 could be a tree or plant, Network 2 might be insects, and Network 3 could be disease organisms.

Nature becomes imbalanced because the interacting network patterns among whole organisms in ecosystems are often compromised. Fragmentation and lack of vitality are the results in the local ecosystem.

CHECK FOR SIGNS OF STRESS OR DECLINE

Dr. Jim talks about stress and decline: What does a stressed tree or plant look like? A tree or plant under stress is trying to sustain itself. It is pulling its Growth Energy inward so it can support at least some growth processes and continue to live. It will let go of some leaves and branches since its Life Force cannot sustain them. This explains why a large tree under stress has a thin canopy and many dead branches at the top. It can only sustain growth in the lower part of the structure.

What is decline? It is generally considered a severely stressed tree exhibiting many of the following characteristics.

Follow these guidelines (from less to more severe)

- *Lackluster look or drooping leaves*
- *Not flowering or fruiting as it did previously*
- *Yellow or curling leaves*
- *Less or smaller leaves overall*
- *Dropping leaves before autumn or not leafing out with others in spring*
- *Thin canopy of leaves, especially in the upper crown of the tree*
- *Signs of insects or diseases*
- *Lots of small, dead branches, especially but not exclusively in the upper crown of the tree*
- *Larger dead or falling branches*

STRESS LEADS TO DECLINE

Dr. Jim underlines the most important points: Trees and plants have built-in responses to stressors, but those responses can't always result in good health. When they are stressed, trees' health is compromised and trees compensate internally. They dedicate their precious and sometimes limited inner resources to compensate for stress.

Because their internal functionality is compromised by stress, they have to burn up more energy to accomplish their normal functions. More energy used for compensating means less energy available for new growth. Thus, trees that are stressed exhibit less growth.

The less that trees and plants add new growth, the further into decline they may slip.

HEADED INTO DECLINE: THE LARCH'S STORY

Dr. Jim draws a distinction about causes: Many people think that to cure their own health, they need to know the cause of their malady. However, I do not have to know a cause of a tree's inner malfunctions. If I get information about a stress factor through my intuition, that is sometimes helpful but not necessary. The apparent cause—such as a stress factor—and the remedy are not necessarily connected when doing bioenergy healing with a tree. It is enough to simply know that there are a multitude of stress factors that compromise trees' inner health.

Dr. Jim describes the Larch's compromised functionality: A Larch tree is a kind of evergreen. This one in Fair Haven, New Jersey, is easily fifty feet tall. To the casual observer, it looked great. But, in my intuitive listening, I could hear the tree say, "Help me. I am hurt." It was pushing out sap in three places.

If a tree has not been recently injured but begins to leak fluids through its bark, that is a sign that circulation is not running properly. If the fluids can't flow up and down, the tree pushes them out. When the circulation system is blocked, the tree pushes sap out through a path of least resistance—old pruning holes, old injuries, or cracks in the bark.

I would like to outline how this Larch's functionality was compromised. I discover this level of detail because I have extensive botanical knowledge. When Basia and I teach Tree Whispering®, there is no need for people to know anything other than roots, truck, branches, leaves, buds, and cells, as parts of trees and plants. Tree Whispering is designed to be a simple and easy permission-based system to help trees.

As for this example with the Larch, please remember that every tree is different! So, what I say about this tree applies only to it.

Written in priority order, these are the functions compromised and specific processes weakened or nonfunctional for the Larch.

1) Circulation in the tree was not operating properly. Since fluids could not move properly up and down in the tree, they were being pushed out or were leaking out of the bark in three places.

2) Specifically, movement up of fluids in the xylem was not occurring.

3) Connection between soil and roots was crippled.

4) Downward movement of fluids in the phloem was blocked.

5) The right reactions were not taking place to convert food (made by photosynthesis) into usable components.

6) The process of photosynthesis was operating at minimal levels (due to circulation issues) and needed to be maximized.

7) The process of photosynthesis was detached from the process that balances plant chemistries in the sap, therefore allowing the out-of-balance sap to block the circulation system.

8) The flow of Growth Energy (which prompts and regulates growth) around the whole structure was unevenly distributed.

9) Life Energy was in a downward spiral leading toward decline.

Dr. Jim concludes: These were only some of the Larch's many compromised internal functions. This Larch was headed into full decline and would have died.

But, weakened inner processes can be rejuvenated.

Systems and other operations that are broken inside of trees and plants can be returned to health.

It is possible.

The wonder is that we can see these trees and not wonder more.

RALPH WALDO EMERSON
AMERICAN LECTURER, ESSAYIST, AND POET, 1803–1882

Keep close to Nature's heart... and break clear away, once in awhile, and climb a mountain or spend a week in the woods. Wash your spirit clean.

JOHN MUIR
AMERICAN NATURALIST, EXPLORER, AND WRITER, 1838-1914

Every creature is better alive than dead, men and moose and pine trees, and he who understands that will rather preserve its life than destroy it.

HENRY DAVID THOREAU
AMERICAN AUTHOR, NATURALIST, AND PHILOSOPHER, 1817–1862

God has cared for these trees, saved them from drought, disease, avalanches, and a thousand tempests and floods. But he cannot save them from fools.

JOHN MUIR
AMERICAN NATURALIST, EXPLORER, AND WRITER, 1838-1914

Only when the last tree has died and the last river has been poisoned, and the last fish has been caught will we realize we cannot eat money.

CREE INDIAN PROVERB

Insight 3:
It Is Possible to Save
Trees or Plants in Decline

Dr. Jim highlights: Why is it possible to save a tree in decline with my holistic, hands-on, biofield-healing, no-product, green-friendly, and sustainable approach?

First, I am not adding stress to the tree since I don't add products or do invasive techniques. Therefore, the tree or any plant doesn't need to use up precious resources to break down the components of those products.

Second, my focus is on restoring the dynamic balance within the tree's internal condition—its state of health—through the use of biofield healing techniques. The techniques are similar to those that work for people in hospitals that include integrative or complementary holistic techniques in their programs.

Third, most importantly, I usually discover that the tree wants to live because I ask it. So, my bioenergy healing techniques serve to set up the conditions within its bioenergy field so that *it can heal itself.*

Bioenergy treatments give the tree or plant a chance to turn around its flow of Life Force from a declining or pulling-in pattern to a growing or pushing-out pattern. Decline can be reversed. Declining trees and plants that I have treated are here to tell the tale.

DECLINING TREES CAN BE SAVED: COPPER BEECH TREE IN PARK

Dr. Jim and the Beech: In a lovely Long Island, New York, town, the curators of a park asked me to save a Copper Beech tree that was already ribboned for removal. The tree was very sick, but they were tree lovers. They would not allow it to be taken down, if it had a chance to live. When they found me, it was already early December, so the tree had already lost the few leaves they told me it had that year.

Normally, if I were to treat a tree in December, my work would wake it up from dormancy. So I usually don't treat trees at that time. However, this particular tree was fighting to regain its health rather than going to sleep as it should have. It would not have survived the winter. So, I was still able to interact with it and heal it.

The tree's circulation was stuck. The tree could not go into dormancy; it was fighting to live. In order for me to help unblock its circulation system, which is the flow of fluids in the xylem and phloem, I had to get the circulation moving again and get the plant chemistry to clear up. I accomplished this clearing of the chemistry in the bioenergy field of the tree but not by physically doing anything to the tree.

I have to interact with the tree's bioenergy field in such a way that I rearrange its allocation of energies so that there is a little *extra* available to it. Then, it can drive its circulation and its own process of clearing the plant chemistry. Once the circulation was cleared, the Beech went into dormancy by itself. It contained within its design intelligence and formation dynamics the *knowledge* or *memory* that it had some renewed circulation with which to drive its inmost processes the following spring. It could now go to sleep for the winter.

Dr. Jim reports: The Copper Beech tree did survive the winter and started to recover the next spring. I checked on it often, giving it tune-up treatments. By August, nine months after my first healing treatment, it showed good foliage on the limbs that were still alive. Of course, dead limbs will not grow new leaves. The curators told me that its leaves were a bit bigger and more plentiful. They agreed to postpone any pruning so no additional stress would be put on the tree. I gave it another healing treatment in autumn so that it would go into dormancy properly again and to prepare it for the extremes of winter.

Sixteen months after the original treatment, the tree was flourishing. Leaves were even bigger and more abundant. After the dead wood was pruned out by a professional tree service, the curators enthusiastically agreed that it looked a lot healthier.

Since its recovery, it has shed older branches on its own and pushed out new branches close to its trunk. The Beech has told me that it was literally becoming a new tree. All trees' growth patterns want to take the path of least resistance.

COPPER BEECH EXPLAINS: I use less energy growing new branches. I'll get rid of these old, useless branches and just grow new ones.

Dr. Jim explains what the tree said: The tree can push out new growth more easily on younger tissue than it can add new growth onto older, compromised limbs. The bigger limbs that are further up in the structure have too much unusable tissue. The tree looks much smaller than it did, but it is still old and wise.

DECLINING TREES CAN BE SAVED: NEVER TOO OLD

Dr. Jim talks about the Native Dogwood: One of the board members of a house of worship in a New Jersey town is a deeply committed environmentalist, organic gardener, and tree lover. It troubled her that the majority of people on the board decided to take down the old and declining Native Dogwood tree in front of their building. She found me, The Tree Whisperer, just in time and called saying, "They want to cut it down next week! They think it's too old. I would hate to have someone tell me that I'm too old and I should be taken down."

Basia and I agree with her wholeheartedly! Trees do decline, but they rarely get "too old." "Too old" is often an excuse that people will use to cut down a tree that they don't like.

"Too old" is an excuse overused by some tree care professionals, too. Don't accept it as an excuse! Don't give up on a sick tree, unless it is a hazard to people or a building. An older tree in decline can be saved, if you can communicate with it and understand its inner workings.

I asked the board members of the house of worship to give my services a try and to give the tree a chance. They did, on both counts. The tree recovered beautifully. It grew robustly for the remainder of the season. Years later, it is still gracing their building's entrance.

DECLINING TREES CAN BE SAVED: TOO MUCH SALT

Dr. Jim frowns: At a Greenwich, Connecticut, property, the snowplow truck broadcast salt crystals right into a mature, hundred-yard-long Hemlock tree hedge and burned the needles right off. Salt that fell to the ground went into solution and was taken up by the roots. By spring, every tree in the hedge was browning, especially at about six feet high where it was hit directly by the salt. The hedge was in decline, looking terrible. I did my proprietary bioenergy healing treatment.

At the end of my treatments, I always check with the treated trees and plants; I ask whether they will need any conventional care to support new growth after they heal internally and after they begin to show signs of new growth.

The response from this Hemlock hedge was that it would accept the addition of some organic compost to its soil to build up the microbial activity that had been destroyed by the salt. But, it didn't want that right away. As a community, the trees of the hedge specified a wait-time of exactly five weeks before adding the *organic compost*—not mulch.

I told the homeowner "June 1st and not before!"

The hedge also wanted some natural fertilizer three weeks after the addition of the organic compost. Organic compost and natural fertilizer may be sensible treatments to support a tree or plant *after* it has gone through some of its inner healing process.

But, always ask the Green Being first from your heart.

At the five-week point after my treatment, *before* any conventional care was applied, the happy homeowner called to tell me how good the Hemlock hedge already looked. It had put on new growth and was beginning to fill in. She also mentioned that a local landscaper stopped her while she was walking her dog. The landscaper wanted to know what she did to the hedge. He saw it when it was all brown and was stunned at its recovery. She told him about my treatment.

DECLINING PLANTS CAN BE SAVED: CORN REBOUNDS IN IOWA

Dr. Jim smiles: Crop fields aren't flat, even in Iowa, which is pretty flat. Most acreage rolls gently. Corn in low-lying areas can suffer decline after heavy rains because the corn stands in water for extended periods of time. That corn becomes stunted. The stunting shows that it is in decline. Generally, waterlogged corn never fully recovers. Even after the water dries up and the corn resumes growing, the corn doesn't catch up in size or in yield to the high-ground corn. It's a financial loss for the grower.

I was called out to look at a four-acre area of organic corn that was stunted due to extended waterlogged conditions. After my bioenergy treatment, this corn rebounded. Its decline was reversed. The grower was thrilled! He said, "I never saw corn do this. The corn came back extremely fast, caught up in size, and yielded as well as the rest."

DECLINE CAN BE REVERSED: CANADIAN BOTANICAL GARDEN WITH MALAYSIAN TREE IN A GREENHOUSE

Dr. Jim recounts the tale: Basia and I were teaching a workshop in Toronto, Canada, one spring. To practice some of the techniques, we led the students to a botanical garden's greenhouse. The curator begged us, "Could you do *anything* to save this tree?"

The tree was from Malaysia, as a part of their tropical collection. I touched it and found that there was still life in it. "Never too late to save a living tree," I told her.

In the previous months, the Malaysian tree had undergone four major stress factors that the curator and I identified.

First, in the middle of winter, the building's heating system went out. During the repair, the weather became bitterly cold, too cold for this heat-loving tree.

Second, she explained that it was customary to spray a very weak alcohol solution on plants for insect control. The botanical garden will not use commercial insecticides to avoid any risk to visitors. But, someone on her staff mistakenly added too much alcohol to the water. Alcohol will sting your skin; think about how it might feel directly on the tree's leaves.

The soil this Malaysian tree was planted in was not of optimal quality nor native to it. Poor soil made a third stress.

The fourth and last stress was a stress produced by love. The staff really wanted the tree to survive. Everyone watered it—a lot. Overwatering is as harmful as underwatering.

Dr. Jim reviews: I have already talked about the fact that stress is additive in trees and that three or more stress factors can lead to decline. When the first stress factor occurs, a plant's natural feedback loops compensate. This compensation is usually not visible in the tree's outer appearance. It would be like taking a simple round-the-block detour when you're driving through town. It slows you down, but you easily resume the trip.

The second stress factor comes along for a tree. It continues to compensate. Now, the effects of that compensation are sometimes visible. For example, in the Northeast United States in two successive years, the weather was unusually warm through December and early January and then the temperatures plummeted. Sugar Maple trees and the Dogwoods had dramatic reactions to those two difficult winters. Most became thin and weak; many Dogwoods didn't bloom much in spring because they had already used most of their flower buds in January.

By the time the third or fourth stress factors come along, the natural processes inside of a plant can no longer compensate. The third or fourth stress factors block the compensations already in place. They compromise the compensations that already occurred. The tree can't adapt to this additional stress and starts to decline, looking sicker and sicker.

Since the tree or plant is weak, maybe insects or diseases come along to take advantage of it for their own necessary life purposes. At this point, insect or disease control methods may be senseless. Insect or disease damage is secondary to the main problem: inner weakness, compensation in functionality, and compromised systems in the tree. At this point, the tree is trapped and can no longer compensate. It needs to find a clear path around the blocked feedback loops, but it can't. Then, it eats up its own resources, has no more food left, and dies.

To save a tree in decline, here's the formula: repair the inner functionality. But, surgery can't be done on a tree's circulation like a stint implant or heart bypass can be done on a person. That's why my hands-on bioenergy healing techniques fit so well with trees and plants. When inner functionality is healed—repaired bioenergetically—there is a reversal of the *eating itself up* downward flow of energy. Whatever energy is left, turns upward to renew operations and kick-start growth.

The compromised parts and systems that *can* work again, *do*. Then, growth drives healing, which then drives growth which then drives more healing and on and on. Full functionality is restored along with the necessary Growth Energy to give the tree a chance to be healthy again. It can survive and thrive.

From my vantage point inside of the tree, the healing is like repairing a spider's web. Imagine a spider's web with a big hole in it. Then, imagine that strands can be taken, one by one, and put back into the right place. The challenge is in teasing the jumbled strands apart and reconnecting them into the right places. People often ask me how I heal trees. The talent is not in making the so-called healing connections. The art is in identifying which ones go where.

Dr. Jim continues with the story: I stood with the Malaysian tree in Toronto to talk through a demonstration of the healing process for the students in that workshop. Of course, everything had to happen in priority order. Its xylem and phloem needed repair. Then, the ability of the tree to get water and nutrients from the roots up to the growing points or leaf buds was restored, while reestablishing the tree's ability to produce food.

At this point, something took me by surprise. Luckily, I was still holding the tree as in the photograph to the left.

In my deep sensory perception, I felt the tree shift its energy upward.

That reversal from *pulling in* Life Energy to *pushing out* Life Energy happened and I felt it immediately.

The tree wanted to grow again!

That reversal or shift of Life Force always happens if a tree was in decline. It just doesn't always happen on cue or while I am standing there.

Sometimes students feel it when they are practicing the techniques. A tree that is going to survive will change the direction of its bioenergy flow. Then, it will grow again!

Before we left, I gave the staff a couple pieces of practical advice: "Don't water it so much," and "Be patient."

How did it turn out for this tree and the people?

Dr. Jim tells how it turned out: I left Toronto with great satisfaction. Because its energy had shifted upward, I knew with total certainty that the tree would survive.

What I didn't know was how long it would take for the tree to begin to put on new growth.

Several months later, I headed back to Toronto without even a phone-call. I knew the Malaysian tree survived. When I got there—sure enough—it was flourishing. The skeletons of its few sick leaves were still there among the lush new canopy.

The curator told her side of the story. She said it seemed to just sit there for many weeks, then all of a sudden, she said it went "Whoosh." She threw her arms apart!

"New leaves came out like crazy," she said. "It began to flourish once again and we were all so happy!"

Her patience paid off. She was glad she waited long enough for the tree to finish turning around its inner processes and to begin showing new growth.

Dr. Jim sums up: After months of growth, she had a different problem. However, this problem was a lot less serious. She worried that as winter was approaching, she would have to trim off some of the leaves that were touching the glass so that the whole tree would not be injured by the cold. I figured that was a nice problem to have after almost losing that tree.

That is proof: It's never too late to save a declining tree or plant. Remember, it still has Life Force in it. Never give up.

Insight 4:
Trees and Plants *Are* Their Goals

Dr. Jim explains: Trees and plants *are* their goals. Sometimes their goals are related to their own health, such as to be healthy or to be strong. Sometimes their goals are related to their Life Force, such as to grow vigorously or to put on more leaves. Their goals could be to enhance their own situation, such as to be the centerpiece of the yard. Or, their goals could be to correct a human error, such as to overcome severe or improper pruning.

Trees and plants don't have goals or think goals. They *are* their goals. What people would call trees' or plants' "goals" are multidimensional energies infused within their current Life Energy and infrastructure.

Many people hold the belief that a goal is something to strive for. In some cases, this is correct. But, what if the goal existed in the same time and same space dimension as our current situation? Suppose that all we had to do was to emotionally and energetically connect to the goal that already was in the same timeframe as our current situation?

For trees, their current situation always lives inside their goal. And conversely, at the same time, the goal lives inside their current situation. It's a fluid condition; it's nonlinear. Therefore, the two-way connection of the current situation and the future is made. It is in two directions. As the goal becomes a physical reality, the relationship of the goal and current situation does not change. If people did that, we wouldn't be striving toward our goals; we would be allowing the goals to occur. It would be a two-way connection between the current situation and the future, bringing those two pieces together. Within the current situation exists the future, and within the future exists the tree's or plant's current situation.

Dr. Jim chuckles: If you don't understand this, ask a tree. It may reveal its reality to you. However, you might have to stand there for a couple of days with it.

GOALS: THE BLUE BLUE SPRUCE IN RUMSON, NEW JERSEY

Dr. Jim remembers: In September, I was called to a property in Rumson, New Jersey, by an arborist concerned about the health of a Blue Spruce on a small estate. It was about 25 feet tall and probably 18 to 20 years old. The arborist had been trying for years to turn its health around since the tree held a key position in the yard. By September—very late in the growing season—the Blue Spruce was looking very brown, not blue at all. By September, it is usually hard to see improvement in a tree since it is preparing to go into dormancy. Also, I faced a quadruple problem with the owner: he was unsatisfied with the arborist's work, still had a sick tree in a key position, didn't want to wait until the next spring to see results, and didn't believe in my bioenergy healing work.

With the arborist's prompting, I proceeded with my Green Centrics™ treatment. In the network patterns of the tree's bioenergy field, I perceived that its plant chemistry—its biochemical processes and enzymatic reactions as well as the ratio of water, nutrients, and sugars flowing in its fluids—was not organized, coordinated, or synchronized. I also perceived that the vascular system, which carries the fluids, showed many blockages of tissue. Imagine if ketchup were mixed with crystalized honey and white school glue. Yuck. Then imagine trying to squeeze that mixture through a bent straw. Impossible. That was the situation the Blue Spruce faced.

In order to clear this situation—to reestablish the proper flow of the biochemical processes, to correct the ratio of fluid constituents, and to break up the blockages—I use only my conscious intention, focused attention, and my proprietary bioenergy healing techniques. I do not apply products.

Dr. Jim specifies: In the language of my treatment notes and records, I "cleared" the plant chemistry's thickness; got the xylem and phloem "opened up," "increased circulation," and adjusted other inner activities necessary for the synergy of the tree's functionality.

I was fortunate to be there when the tree's declining bioenergy flow shifted upward. I felt the *fireworks* of the energy-shift and had a strong feeling in my body that it would have new growth in a matter of time. In fact, later that afternoon, I commented to the estate manager, "Doesn't the tree look better?" He looked at it with a smiling glimmer. Then, he called over one of the workers and said, "Take a look at this tree." The estate worker said, "Yeah! I think he fixed it!"

In the process of performing my Green Centrics™ healing system with the tree, I discovered its goals. Its first goal was to put on new branches and new growth at the tips of existing branches. The second goal was to *fill in*—in other words—to have that new growth fill existing blank spots in its physique. Those goals seemed logical to me. The third goal made me smile. It wanted to be a fully grown *Blue* Blue Spruce. This goal seemed to come from the very *heart* of the tree. The goal sounds to me like a desire to fully express exactly what it is—as a living Being. Those three goals are mutually supportive and can co-exist. Within those goals are included its current situation: very brown in September. The tree made the two-way connection between its current situation and its goals.

Basia interjects: Let me try to say this goal idea in another way. As a human Being, I can understand that I must acknowledge my own current reality in order to move toward something I desire. For example: It would be impossible for me to travel to the store if I did not acknowledge or realize that I was at home, or vice versa. In treating this tree, Dr. Jim realizes that—in its own way—the tree held within its unique tree consciousness a knowledge about its own current situation connected with an understanding of its desired state of health, all at the same time.

Dr. Jim finishes the story: In treating this tree, I learned something about how I approach my goals. Then, I incorporated this insight into the Green Centrics System in my quest to constantly improve it.

The following May, I visited the *Blue* Blue Spruce. Its goals were a visible current reality. It put on substantial new growth despite a cold winter. The new growth was filling in the blank spots and, of course, it was very deep blue. The tree was expressing itself as a fully grown *Blue* Blue Spruce.

GOALS: SMART CABBAGE HEADS AT THE FARM

Dr. Jim reminds: It sounds a bit strange but remember that trees and plants *are* their goals. They don't have goals. The difference in those statements comes from a different relationship with time. They are *being* themselves fully in the moment so both their current circumstances and their goals live together in that multi-dimensional space.

Such was the case with the Cabbages at an organic farm. This was to be an autumn Cabbage crop. When I first saw them in September, the Cabbages were quite small in size, considering that the people intended to harvest them before winter set in. Temperatures in September were already getting cooler and days shorter, which does not favor quick growth.

The innovation for me was that I could perceive the small physical Cabbage head inside of the larger energy biofield of the Cabbage head. The small physical head just had to *fill in* so that they could fully occupy the space that the big biofield head already formed. The goal of the Cabbage was already there within the biofield level.

More than that, the small physical head and the big biofield head were connected. In the process of growing, the small physical Cabbage was already *being* the big Cabbage head. The passage of time within the human dimension would help it to *fill in* within the energetic aspect of the biofield. Since plants don't recognize time and since they *are* their goals, they just grow to fill in the physical level until the physical reality occupies the energetic level of reality. You could say that when they first started to sprout, that *is and was* their goal.

Dr. Jim comments on genetics: Someone might say that the goals are all in the genetics. I say that the genes help support the energetic biofield level that is already formed. Genetics support moving into the energetic or biofield reality. The whole plant at every level holds connections between the physical reality and the energetic reality.

At the farm, those big Cabbage heads fully expressed themselves and were harvested in early December.

Their goal was physically reached.

Insight 5:
Trees and Plants
Operate *In* Community

Dr. Jim, The Tree Whisperer®, draws a distinction: Trees and plants operate in community, but this is *not* just because their roots touch. Trees may operate in community while they are not near enough to each other to have touching roots. Trees and plants of the same species or of similar, nearby species may operate in various layers of community. It may be Oak with other Oaks, Beech with Beeches, Oaks with Beeches, etc.

What makes the community? It is the sharing of signals among individuals. What is this signal that keeps trees and plants operating in community?

Scientists say that it is chemical or hormonal molecules traveling on the wind or in the underground rhizosphere. It is true that plants send out such molecules. *7 & 8*

But that is not the kind of community I am talking about. I believe that community is formed among trees and plants through their *bioenergy field vibrations* or *song*. One member of the community *sings* vibrations to others in the community. It is the same song for similar species. That song is also compatible or in harmony with related species of a larger community. Native Americans have told me that they hear and dance in rhythm to the trees' songs during their ceremonies.

Dr. Jim continues talking about community: Have you heard the expression "can't see the forest for the trees?" Well, people usually can't see the community for the trees. In other words, our idea of what a tree is has been shaped by the cultural notion that this thing with a trunk and branches is the tree. When I say the word "community," you probably think of all these individual things we call "trees" teaming up to work in a group.

I ask you to expand your thinking. Community—the synergy of all those individual trunks with branches and leaves—really acts as the whole tree. Perceiving individual trunks would be like looking at your fingers and thinking that each of them is a separate individual—not seeing your whole hand. Your fingers

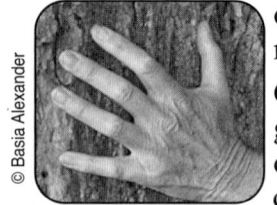

operate in community *as* your hand. It is much the same with trees.

Community among trees and plants is like a group consciousness such as a flock of birds or school of fish. All of the members operate as one. It is the community that is the *whole* tree or plant. Each member of the community sends out a signal or a *song* to the other members. This is how each member stays healthy and continues to *actively* grow. Each member of the community helps other members using the various levels of community. If any member becomes sick, it falls out of community. Why?

To protect the health of the overall group.

Here's an example. When several trees or plants of the same type are transplanted, one or two of them might die. Why did the rest survive? Those that died may have been weak or sick, so they fell out of community in order to protect the others. All trees or plants operate for the good of the community. Other layers of community cross a wide variety of trees and plants on both a physical and biofield level.

Dr. Jim adds: The last question you might have is "How big is the community?" It varies. I believe that communities are like overlapping rings. One community is connected to another, and connected to another. You might think of the symbol of the Olympic rings and how they overlap. I do not know how far communities of trees really go. Like a tsunami wave that touches every shore, communities of trees and plants are potentially enormous. A community may not be infinite, but I believe that, ultimately, all trees form a global community.

After all, we are all connected.

COMMUNITY: THE OLD BEECH AND THE YOUNGSTERS, LONG ISLAND, NEW YORK

Dr. Jim's example of how community works: I told you in Insight # 3 about how well the old Beech tree in the park on Long Island, New York, was recovering. During my many visits, I explained the idea of trees operating in community to the curators. There was an open field around the senior Beech where they wanted to plant more trees.

They asked, "Would the Beech tree like buddies?"

I said, "Yes, of course!"

Their park contained acres of wooded land. The three of us walked into the forest to find small Beech trees that could be transplanted. The curators asked me to prepare three young trees with a healing session before the move so that they wouldn't go into shock. Then, afterward, I did another session to balance them to their much smaller root system. It's hard to get a good root ball when removing trees from a forest.

I discovered that the senior Beech and these three youngsters already started the process of forming a community for themselves. However, the community could not be fully formed because the individuals were still not healthy enough. After additional hands-on bioenergy healing treatments which restored dynamic natural balance to all, I could feel the community forming. Through their stronger songs, I could sense the support that each tree was giving the others.

The senior Beech was giving the three youngsters a sense of groundedness. Since their root systems were so small, the groundedness would help them have a closer connection to Earth, and to put down new roots into the new soil in which they were planted. Then, they could put on new roots faster.

Meanwhile, the three youngsters had that boundless, youthful buoyancy that you see when human children are running around in play. The tree youngsters gave the senior Beech the resilient, full-of-life pep it needed to fuel its own inner healing process.

This is only one example of how community works among trees. Through their sharing of Life Force—their song—every healthy tree or plant bonds in some way with the others nearby. Each supports all the others' growth and well-being.

COMMUNITY: YES, THE OTHER ORANGE TREE IS HERE SOMEWHERE

Dr. Jim recalls: In a lovely Florida backyard, the homeowner showed me her prize Orange tree. It was looking poorly. I set out to do my healing services. At a certain point, the prize Orange tree asked to be reconnected to another Orange tree. When it got sick, it fell out of community with the other. I didn't have to see the other tree in order to make the connection between the two biofields. I had a general sense of it being over-there, somewhere. The two Orange trees would form an Orange tree community. One would help the other stay healthy.

When my healing services were done, I told the woman what happened in the treatment. She declared: "There is no other Orange tree around here! None of my neighbors have Orange trees!" I was confused. The trees are usually right. In her protest, she spoke quite loudly and that must have roused her husband from his slumber in the house. He came outside and walked us to the fence at the far corner. He pointed beyond the immediate neighbor's place and to the other side of their fence. Yes, there it was, the other Orange tree.

COMMUNITY: THE HOTEL LOBBY GANG

Basia adds her story: This was one of those spacious, two-story hotel lobbies. While waiting for Dr. Jim to check out of the hotel on one of our many speaking engagements, I thought I'd have a little chat with a beautiful potted tree. It was not as cordial as I expected. Gruffly, it communicated to me that *they* didn't care about humans because *they* had their own association, right there in the lobby, without anyone knowing about it.

When I looked around, I saw dozens of philodendrons hanging from above the registration desk, a clutch of potted palms on the other side of the door, and many other plants scattered throughout the area. I laughed! There they were—like Martians in our midst—having tea parties, and the people didn't have a clue.

COMMUNITY: KNITTING THE GREENS

Dr. Jim describes his work at a golf course: I was working on a golf course in the Northeast United States that had trouble in the heat and humidity of summer. Some of the grass on the greens died. Some grass remained, but it was spotty. The superintendent roughed up the soil and planted new grass seeds in the dead spots. The new seeds began to germinate and send their new, green sprouts through the soil. I was amazed at how quickly the older, established grass wanted to connect with the sprouting seeds, and vice versa. There were two purposes here. First, the established grass could help the younger seedlings continue to sprout and become established. Second—most importantly—all of the grass could cover the ground, conserve moisture, and shade each other's roots and blades for optimal growth conditions. I felt their urgency to knit together and form a community. That made me believe that all their lives depended on their bonding together and knitting together quickly.

COMMUNITY: MOUNTAINSIDES AND VALLEYS

Dr. Jim and the Lodgepole Pine Trees: Entire mountainsides of Lodgepole Pine Trees have died in Colorado. Conventional interpretation of this blames the Pine Bark Beetle. While expanding beetle populations due to warmer winters were the immediate agents of death, I believe that they were not the authentic cause. Forests suffered a human policy of fire suppression as well as at least nine years of extreme drought following snow-melt. Drought weakened the trees making them more susceptible to the increased beetle populations.

When I first communicated with the innate intelligence of the Lodgepole Pine trees in autumn of 2007, I discovered severe weaknesses within all parts, functions, and systems such as circulation of water/nutrients/sugars, cellular repair/growth, food production with photosynthesis, and others.

The Lodgepole Pine forests in the Vail and Winter Park areas of Colorado are nearly monocultures—meaning that those are the only kinds of trees except for patches of Aspens. This makes them powerful communities. Trees may be aware, at some level, of human property boundaries, but they don't honor human boundaries. So, the Lodgepole's communities are enormous: potentially whole mountainsides and valleys.

I have an ongoing study on three properties in the Vail valley and on 11 properties in the Winter Park/Fraser valley of Colorado. I believe that bioenergy treatments I do on these properties spread exponentially around and eventually overlap because of the powerful community energy that Lodgepole Pine trees share.

The heavily infested trees at the beginning of the study did not survive. But, over the years of this study, health and dynamic balance within functionality were bioenergetically restored to remaining pines. Results included less burrowing beetles and robust new growth in the then-recovering treated trees.

Continuing through autumn of 2012, Lodgepole Pines on the properties showed high survival rates and good growth. Trees show excellent growth with little new incidence of tree decline.

Basia's and my concept called Cooperative BioBalance® was developing over this same time frame. The fundamental principle of Cooperative BioBalance is *live-and-let-live* because all life forms want to live. Cooperative BioBalance is a new field of inquiry and practical techniques through which people form equal and cooperative partnerships with trees, plants, forests, crops, and their related insect and disease organisms. In my research, I am now showing that ecosystems—small and large—can be returned to dynamic balance with the processes of Co-Existence Technologies™.

The study with the Lodgepole Pines afforded me the opportunity to develop my Co-Existence Technologies methods on private homeowner's tracts of land ranging from two acres to more than fifty acres. Through these techniques, I also connected with the Life Force of the Pine Bark Beetles. The insect intelligence said that the insects would simply go to trees that were weak. Strong, healthy, fully functional trees naturally tolerate a few of what is called "beetle hits." Weak trees attract beetles in large numbers and then succumb.

Dr. Jim addresses common questions about these tests: Is this natural reforestation? My systems are permission-based. If I were disturbing a natural process, I would not have been able to treat the trees. They would have said "no" in answer to my question, "Permission to treat?"

Finally, please consider the appearance of the Pine Bark Beetles on Lodgepole Pines in the big picture. Various parts of the United States are having similar problems: Emerald Ash Borer is attacking Ash trees, Bronze Birch Borer is threatening Birches, Oak Wilt is hurting Oaks, Sudden Oak Death is devastating both the Live and Coastal Oaks in California, Aspen Decline is happening in Colorado, and bleeding canker is showing up on Beech trees everywhere. Is all this natural? I doubt it!

Trees are weakening everywhere. When they are weak, they fall out of community, thereby weakening further.

Insight 6:
Plants and Trees Signal for Help—Which Attracts Other Organisms

Dr. Jim talks about signaling: When a tree or plant is sick and falls out of community, it sends out a signal for help. That call for help also attracts insects and disease organisms.

What comes first? The so-called "pest" or the weakened tree?

Weakness in the tree or plant comes first. It is the biofield messages that the Green Being broadcasts about its weakness that attracts most insects and diseases. I believe it is the song they sing and the scents they emit that are the attractants. Only the most aggressive or nonnative insects and diseases will go to healthy trees.

When I use the Green Centrics System™, I plug the sick tree's biofield into its community. When it is restored to the shared biofield of the community, the other trees can help the healing process so that the sick tree can become fully operational. In another sense, the whole community gets the treatment.

Dr. Jim asks: What about when a tree or plant has had an insecticide, fungicide, or other chemical put on it to knock back a pest? I have found that just killing the pests will not stop the tree's call for help. It was the tree's or plant's signal requesting help that attracted the pest in the first place. Healing the internal operations and reconnecting the tree into its community will stop the "help" message from being broadcast by the plant and therefore stop more pests from being attracted.

Without healing the internal operations, the vicious cycle continues. People are tempted to spray again, not knowing that the tree or plant is still sending out the plea for help, which attracts more pests. It is only by restoring the inner operations and rejoining the tree into its community that the vicious cycle can be broken and the tree can be brought back into full health.

SIGNALING: THE WRONG PLANT IN THE WRONG PLACE

Dr. Jim describes: On the South Fork of Long Island, New York, people build large homes at the edge of the beach so that they can see the Atlantic Ocean. But, these homeowners don't want people on the beach or on the roads to see into their homes, so they put in privacy hedges.

This particular property used Privet for their hedge—a small-leafed plant with dense, criss-crossing branches. Privet is usually a vigorously growing plant, but the community of shrubs at this house was just too close to the salt water, salt air, sandy soil, and weather extremes of the beach. Its downward spiral of weakness over several years attracted insects, called Scale, which further defoliated it by crawling along stems and congregating at the base of leaves. When I arrived one spring, I could see right through the hedge in many places.

The plants could not get up and move. The homeowner didn't want to replace them. The only holistic solution was to help the hedge regain its inner health so that it would naturally resist the Scale. Healthy plants naturally resist diseases and insects. Any university extension agent or landscape professional will say the same thing.

I did my bioenergy field healing treatment. I did not use any products whatsoever; nor did the homeowner. When I returned several weeks later, delightful little oval leaves were filling in the bare spots. New, light-green growth was everywhere.

What about the Scale? I examined the new leaves and did not see any sign of the insects. The hedge grew strongly for the remainder of the season.

But, the plant was still in the wrong place. Stress from the weather, the ocean, and the poor soil would add up again. The hedge would need lots of attention with—preferably—organic products and periodic inner strengthening with my bioenergy treatments in order to stay healthy.

Insight 7:
We Are All Connected

Dr. Jim talks about community and connection: We are all fundamentally forms of energy, say the quantum physicists. Therefore, we are all connected in at least that way, if not in a more vast, spiritual way.[9]

I see the truth of this connection through my work with the Life Energy and biofields of trees. And, that is a very spiritual experience for me. In working with the Life Force of trees, I get to see what a fine-tuned instrument they are. When my Life Force is connected with trees' Life Force, it helps me to see that we humans are also fine-tuned instruments. So, how could it be a surprise that two such amazing instruments are connected?

I could talk to you about the sciences, or show you the billions-of-years-old family tree of organisms on Earth, or mention the teachings of various spiritual systems, but I cannot *convince* you that we are all connected. You either know this is true in your own experience of life, or you do not agree. And that is okay.

Tree Whispering® workshops are designed to be experiential. We lead people through guided visualization experiences. We ask people to go outside and touch the trees, feeling their Life Energy and their majesty. People who learn our tree healing techniques report a profound experience of kinship with the trees and plants that they touch. They tell us that they know "we are all connected."

*WE ARE ALL CONNECTED: NEW HOPE AFTER A TERRIBLE MISTAKE
BY A WASHINGTON STATE APPLE GROWER*

Dr. Jim relates a happy ending: On a tour of Northwest Pacific fruit growers, one owner approached me with a gloomy look and a desperate request: "Would you please come to my orchard as soon as possible?"

The previous year, he accidently sprayed the trees in one field with a popular total vegetation control chemical. Intending to use a fungicide, he simply picked up the wrong tank without looking and started spraying. The chemical completely defoliated the trees. Anguish was plaguing him. His trees did not bloom and were very thin and weak. This was not just an income for him. He loved his trees. He was worried about losing future years of production and even losing the trees entirely. He knew he made a mistake that hurt the trees.

First, I interfaced with the trees. Yes, they were sick, but not fatally. My bioenergy work boosted their ability to process out the foreign chemical and to generate more leaves that season so that they could feed themselves. This would put them well on the way to healing themselves.

It was not hopeless, but the grower was in such deep pain over his mistake that he *felt* hopeless. That was the real problem. He kneeled down next to me while I was treating the trees. I explained how I was restoring the trees' interior workings and told him about the steps involved. That was intriguing for him because he didn't know such a thing was possible.

Then, I asked him to put his hands on a tree, close his eyes, and allow himself to receive a sensation or a feeling. Meanwhile, with my hands on the same tree, I communicated to it that the owner was there, too. I told the tree that the owner wanted all the trees to survive and thrive. In a few minutes, we both felt the tree's Life Force. We felt positive activity in the trees. Most of all, by connecting with the trees, the owner felt his hope return for their well-being. He was joyous! He grinned from there to the Mississippi. He was reconnected to the trees emotionally. His hope for the survival of the orchard was restored.

After fearing a loss of years of production because the trees would either limp along or have to be replaced, all turned out well. The following year, there were enough apples for limited production. The year after that, the trees were back in full production and he was a wiser and grateful man. Trees, people, and everything—we are all connected.

WE ARE ALL CONNECTED: FINANCIAL TROUBLES?
JUST ASK THE CORN

Dr. Jim recalls his innovative approach: In the early years of system development, I did a trial on a corn field belonging to a conventional grower, Bill, in New Jersey. He was agreeable to have any bit of help he could get for his corn. As I did my healing treatments on the corn, I had a clear impression that Bill was having some kind of money problems. But, Bill was not the kind of guy I could walk up to and say, "Your corn told me that you are having financial difficulties." That just wouldn't fly. So I decided to try another approach.

I knew from my years in the agricultural chemical business that good farmers take the time to walk through their fields. They look for signs of diseases and insects. They look at the rate of growth. They think about the crop and how they want to market it. I suggested that Bill walk his fields. His reaction was a shock.

"Listen, young man! The price of corn is going down this year. The price of fuel is skyrocketing! I have a stack of bills this high for this corn already." He held his hands two feet apart. "I don't know whether I can afford to harvest it! So you are telling me that I should go out and walk these fields?"

Without a moment's hesitation, I said, "Yes! Listen, just walk a few rows. Look at the corn. Think about it. It's really a good crop. You never know what kind of idea you might come up with to market your harvest."

And so he did. Not only did he walk the fields, but he also had an excellent harvest. The best result was his new idea. Instead of taking his corn to traditional markets for pennies, he decided he would shuck and bag the corn for wild animal feed. The following year, he bought a bagging machine because he was doing so well.

WE ARE ALL CONNECTED: HELPING TREES IN HURRICANE SANDY

Basia tells the story: Dr. Jim and I heard about Hurricane Sandy on Wednesday, October 24th, 2012. By Thursday, it was still in the Caribbean, but forecasts were dire for the East Coast of the USA. We knew we had to do something. So we created the Storm Prep Whispers™ and emailed them on Friday morning. They spread from e-list to e-list like wild-fire. We think it was because people realized "we are all connected" and wanted to help their trees. Hundreds, perhaps thousands, of people offered the Storm Prep Whispers to their dear trees in the path of oncoming Hurricane Sandy.*10*

People had so much success with helping and saving their trees in the stricken areas of New Jersey, New York, and Connecticut, that we assembled their stories in a fund-raising book about it.

People Saving Their Trees in Hurricane Sandy: TreeProtector.org
contains the inspiring, heartfelt, and heroic stories of the brave
people—in their own words—who used the Tree Whispering®
Storm Prep Whispers™ to help their trees survive and to
empower themselves in the face of disaster.*11*

Here is a brief sampling of what the heroes said:

"This was one positive thing I could do in the face of feeling so much helplessness
in the storm."   —*Liz Wassell, Reiki for Animals, New Paltz, New York*

"Thank you for giving me the instructions to help my trees. Storm Prep Whispers
need to spread throughout the world to help all our dear trees."
—*Rachel McPherson, Founder of The Good Dog Foundation and author of*
Every Dog Has A Gift, Red Hook and Brooklyn, New York

"As an Arborist, I used The Storm Prep Whispers. They are beautiful and
integrated messages. I wish I had a bullhorn in my car so I could say
them everywhere."
—*David Slade, Licensed Arborist, Family Tree Care, Guilford, Connecticut*

"I know the Storm Prep Whispers really helped my family of trees stay safe."
—*Janet Nicoll, Accountant, Hamilton Square, New Jersey*

"We thank Dr. Jim and Basia for preparing our property for Hurricane Sandy. It
was worthwhile and it definitely worked—our trees are fine. We are so grateful."
—*Alison Iati, Teacher, Randolph, New Jersey*

"I am so grateful that on my block and a few blocks around us, we had very little
tree damage."   —*Pat Anderson, Teacher, Rockville Centre, Long Island, New York*

"Thank you for your wise instruction. I believe it was this work that saved
my trees."
—*Ellie Corda, Massage Therapist and Reiki Master, Hackettstown, New Jersey*

"Your Whispers helped me prepare physically, but more importantly, emotionally
for the storm, and for the aftermath in my area that was hit very hard by
Hurricane Sandy."   —*Shelagh W., Mountain Lakes, New Jersey*

"We are all in this together. Thank you for your continual support of
our ecosystem!"
—*Laura Parisi, Food Shaman and Reiki Master, Old Greenwich, Connecticut*

"The Whispers were taken to heart, spoken, and heard. The trees I love still stand."
—*Jennifer Pettit, Prenatal/Postpartum Yoga Instructor, New York City, New York*

"People can help their trees and people can collaborate with Nature. These are the
key messages Dr. Jim and Basia are successfully carrying into exciting times!"
—*Sylvie Oliva, Flight Attendant and Geomancer, Phoenix, Arizona*

Insight 8:
To Solve Any Situation, Come from the Tree's or Plant's Point of View

Basia illuminates: What do Dr. Jim and I mean when we say, "come from the tree's point of view?"

Let me ask you, what does it mean to come from anyone's point of view? Perhaps your spouse, child, friend, or a coworker has said, "Gee, if you could see it through my eyes, then you would understand." That's what we mean. But, trees don't have eyes, they have roots. You have to feel as if you are standing in their roots, trunk, and branches, looking out at the scene from one stationary place.

I think that I shall never see a poem as lovely as a tree.

A tree whose hungry mouth is pressed against the earth's sweet flowing breast.

A tree that looks at God all day and lifts her leafy arms to pray.

A tree that may in summer wear a nest of Robins in her hair, upon whose bosom snow has lain, who intimately lives with rain.

Poems are made by fools like me but only God can make a tree.

TREES, BY ALFRED JOYCE KILMER (1913)

Mr. Kilmer stepped into the tree's world and felt what its life must be like. He told us that he understood its Divinity and appreciated it in the best way he could: iambic tetrameter and rhyming couplets.[12]

Basia talks about asking questions and getting messages: Throughout this book, Dr. Jim has talked about asking questions of trees and plants. Asking questions is how he does his work. The questions he poses in his heart are answered by the trees through his intuition. This process helps him come from their point of view. On page 5 of this book, I offered suggestions for having a personal experience of connection and communication with a Green Being. On page 13, there is a list of ways you can cultivate receiving nonverbal information from trees and plants.

Once you have made the connection and are coming from the tree's or plant's point of view, you'll feel a greater trust. If you start asking the tree or plant questions from your heart, you will get information or messages.

Four Categories of Messages

1) What's going on for the Green Being's health. This includes
(a) what is going on inside of its physiology and/or
(b) what are environmental conditions that influence the tree or
plant on either the inside or outside.

2) Instructions to people. These are actions to take, such as
"water, now" or "stop watering so much."

3) Personal messages for you. Get information that is useful in your
personal life such as "spend more time breathing deeply" or
"bring your children to visit me."

4) Insights or wisdom from Spirit; timeless information or advice.

Basia continues about asking "yes" and "no" questions:
Asking trees and plants anything is like playing the game of 20 Questions. Even if you think it's silly, when you ask another living Being a question you will get a response. You may feel "yes" or "no" feelings. You might actually hear those answers in your inner hearing. Or, the answer might come as a visual image or in the form of an impression or emotion.

We are accustomed to speaking a verbal language. However, our bodies have their own language. Remember the advice you got in school for true/false tests? It probably was: "Always take your first answer." I believe that is because you can feel a "yes" or "no" response within your body when you make a true or false statement.

Dr. Jim asks you a question: Could the plant actually tell you "no"? It could. And if it does, I would say to you, "respect that answer." Hearing a "no" answer does not have to fly in the face of your self-confidence or your agenda.

The plant's "no" answer may be a guidance system leading you to a different way. Ask the plant's bioenergy field and innate intelligence some more questions. A "no" answer could mean "not now, but maybe later," or it could mean "do it another way."

For example: "Don't transplant me now, I'm stressed" or "Organic fertilizer in two weeks, not now." I have found that many trees that have been under stress need to recuperate before they can be transplanted or tolerate a product. It's like us: If you have just had the flu, you might not want to sit down to a big steak and potatoes dinner right away.

Generally, trees and plants are willing to work with us. You will probably be able to do what you want, but it may not be exactly your way. Be open to a different way. Let the plant or tree explain it to you with this yes-or-no language or by intuitive knowings. Trust the path.

Dr. Jim's experience with "no" to treatment: My systems are permission-based. I *always* ask a tree or plant if it wants a treatment. What I *don't* do is expect to get a predictable answer based solely on my professional training. Professional training teaches that identifiable conditions require certain answers or prescribe certain actions. Since what I do is beyond conventional diagnosis, I have no preference or agenda when I approach a tree. More than that, I have learned to check my ego at the door.

I know that trees are *not* like stubborn children. "No" is a piece of good information that leads me to be more creative and insightful because I have to keep asking more carefully worded and deeper questions until I get a better understanding. A "yes" leads me to the next phase of questioning or leads me to clarity.

Rarely—perhaps six or seven times since I started—has a tree said "no" to treatment because it didn't want to regain health. Most Green Beings have a natural force to live. But, sometimes, a tree is so sick that it communicates to me that I should leave it alone. So, I give it a blessing and let Nature take its course.

Dr. Jim comments on professionals and their clients: Generally, professionals in tree and plant care are reluctant to ask a tree or plant a question about its well-being since the answer might contradict what their client wants. However, the professionals who work with me and who practice my systems find that their clients are happier. Why? Because their clients' trees and plants are healthier. Also, those professionals get repeat business from clients. Enlightened homeowners prefer professionals who care about saving trees and plants. We are finding that more homeowners want tree care professionals who are not only knowledgeable but also are passionate tree lovers. Clients appreciate when their tree-care people are on the leading edge of futuristic advances as well as looking out for the best interests of their whole properties.

If you hire someone to take care of your trees and plants, then the insights you are gaining in this book will help you to direct them in their work. We encourage you to ask your professionals whether they can step inside of your trees' and plants' world.

Basia encourages stepping inside the plant's world: Stepping inside a tree's world is a special, and sometimes life-altering experience. We offer written and audio guided visualization exercises to help anyone do that. Once people are inside the tree's world, people are coming from the tree's point of view.

TREE'S POINT OF VIEW: FLY UP TO GET THE BIRD'S EYE VIEW

Basia shares one of her secrets: I like to visit notable and large trees. Before I go—or before Dr. Jim makes a house call to a large property—the Internet is my first stop.

I plug the address into one of the mapping sites then zooooom way in on the satellite view. To come from the trees' perspective, I ignore the roads and the buildings. That lets me see how they interrelate in community and with the land. For me, that's a good first step in coming from the tree's point of view.

Check out a few trees just for fun. Search on *Santa Barbara, California, Moreton Bay Fig Tree*, or *Tane Mahuta, Waipoua Forest, Waipoua Kauri Forest, Northland, New Zealand*, or *Fortingall Yew tree, Fortingall Church, Perthshire, Scotland*, and go to the satellite view. Just look at how big they are from the bird's eye view.

TREE'S POINT OF VIEW: GROWING UP INTO SALTY BREEZES

Dr. Jim recalls the trees in Fair Haven, New Jersey: The Maple trees were living near a river bank, not far from the river's outlet to the ocean. They were showing signs of environmental stress. I sought the cause of the stress by asking the trees. They told me that when they were young, their leafy crowns were protected from the salt breezes.

Coming from the trees' point of view, this made sense. They could have been protected by nearby houses and other trees.

They told me that as they grew older, their leafy canopies grew above the houses and taller than other trees. The salt breezes from the ocean were now causing stress.

The breezes can't be stopped, but the trees' physiologies can be balanced to the factor and healed. The treatment would keep the trees healthy in spite of salt breezes blowing on them.

TREE'S POINT OF VIEW: THE YO-YO OF NOT ENOUGH THEN TOO MUCH WATER

Dr. Jim describes the situation at a housing development: On the east end of Long Island, New York, a developer transplanted 27 Linden trees, all in a row. By the time I was asked to work at the property, they were in their locations for about two years. I could tell that they were not healthy trees when they were originally transplanted. I got there in the heat of summer with temps in the upper 90s and low 100s Fahrenheit. At first, the Lindens were dry and showed signs of wilting. Then the watering system was turned on. The soil got too wet and Phytophthora, a disease organism, set in.

LINDEN TREES AT DEVELOPMENT SITE, LONG ISLAND: We are weak! We are trying to get water into the leaves. Our leaves wilt because they don't get enough water. Then, too much water is at our roots! Our roots are sitting in water! The disease in the soil comes alive and colonizes our roots. Now we have bleeding spots on our trunks.

Do not put chemicals on us. We would have to diffuse them and that would take our precious energy. We are not sure if we have enough strength to do that. How will we survive?

Dr. Jim explains what the Lindens were saying: The Lindens were not healthy to begin with. Excess heat and no rain caused their inner feedback cycles to slow down. Circulation had nearly shut down and photosynthesis was inhibited. So, what little food the trees were producing was not moving to create new growth.

It was already late August when I started to heal these trees. I'll give a few of the treatment details in case you're curious. The plant chemistry needed clearing. Then, it was important to get the little food that the trees were able to produce to move around in the tree, again. With that food moving around and breaking down, fuel would be produced for the trees' operations, such as circulation. Having circulation moving would, in turn, connect the feedback loop to get food moving around and breaking down to create even more energy for the trees. With a return to healthy operations, the trees could naturally resist the effects of the disease organism.

Dr. Jim asks: See how everything is connected when you come from the tree's point of view?

More energy and especially increased circulation would help drive photosynthesis. Therefore, maximizing the photosynthesis processes became a priority. I had to connect to the feedback loop to make more food. More food would increase energy production and, thus, more energy production would increase circulation. Everything needed to be operating in sequence and then simultaneously. Go ahead and try to visualize this in three dimensions because a tree is a multi-dimensional Being. By late September, the Lindens were regaining their health and the canker spots were beginning to clear.

Tree's Point of View: Effects of Drought While Water Is Everywhere

Dr. Jim talks about dehydration: At the same developer's Long Island property, seven Holly trees were transplanted the previous year. With the onset of summer, they weren't getting enough water. Their roots hadn't had a chance to grow outside of their burlap-covered root balls when the extreme temperatures hit. They went into "shut down," as you might say of a person in cardiac arrest. Leaf buds dried out on larger branches. Smaller branches were also drying up. There was no new leaf development and they were looking very thin.

Of course, the developer—a tree-loving man—had the watering system going but the trees weren't getting enough. Just like any tree after a drought, their exquisitely designed inner operations shut down. When a tissue of any kind—plant or human—is *hydrated*, that means that the water can easily transfer across the cell wall and operate in balance with all the interior cell structures. When a cell becomes *dehydrated*, its wall is no longer as permeable, and the inner structures shrink. My first bioenergy healing priority was rehydrating the xylem and phloem—the *fluid transport tubes* themselves. Sadly, we can't just hook up an intravenous solution in a tree's branch like we can in a person's arm. These inner *pipes* are fragile tissues, only a few cells across. They are as delicate as a china cup. You can't hit them with a metaphorical sledge hammer. As I stood with my hands on a larger branch of one of the Hollies, I noted that the tone of its communication to me was fragile-sounding.

What was the Holly's point of view?

HOLLY TREES AT DEVELOPMENT SITE, LONG ISLAND: Ask my friend Water to visit me. But ask that he come like breath, as a vapor. He will come as a thief in the night. He will slip into my cells quietly and slowly. Ask the earthen hardness of my cells to soften and give way. The walls will yield if you will surround them with a softening Light. Then, ask my friend Air to step aside so that Water might take its place inside my tubes. This will be a relief to me. Then, I can drink, but only a little. Slowly. Slowly.

Allow my friend Water to do his job as a bearer. Ask him to carry food and deliver himself into my arms and to my good children at the ends of my arms. My buds are dried up and I cannot cry for them. But the Fire in the Water will revive them. Ask my friend Fire to move quickly into new leaves. Ask Air to join Fire in my leaves. They will work together. Then, Water will carry. More children at the ends of my arms will grow. Thank you for your help.

Dr. Jim interprets what the Hollies were saying: In their symbolic but very moving communication, the Hollies were telling me how to get their circulation systems going from their point of view. Using my knowledge of the Four Classical Elements—Earth, Air, Fire, and Water—the metaphors were the trees' way of telling me to use what I would call "hydrating" bioenergies. In this way, they told me to first hydrate the cells of the xylem and phloem *tubes* from the tips of the roots to the ends of the branches. Then, fluids—which could be drawn up from the roots—could move as continuous streams all the way to the buds at the ends of the branches.

Whatever food they could make inside of their existing leaves could then be transported—especially to leaf buds—in order to get cells dividing again. Any leaf buds that could be rehydrated would provide even more food-energy to support establishment of a new growing↔healing cycle. Then—and only then—I asked the developer to turn up the watering system.

At first, when the water was turned up, their exquisitely designed natural operations could not gear-up to take advantage of the presence of water. It's like leading a horse to water, but he won't drink. In this case, the Hollies *couldn't* drink right away. As they began to incorporate the healing treatment, their ability to assimilate and use the water increased. After about three weeks, tiny new leaves appeared at the ends of branches.

Later, the Hollies told me that the soil they were living in wasn't acidic enough. They asked me to lower the pH. That confirmed soil testing that was done earlier without my knowledge. The Hollies added that the developer should not attempt to lower the pH for another three to four weeks, until they had healed.

Evenutally, they told me they were ready for the soil around them to be more acidic. The timing of the soil amendment was crucial so that it didn't put stress onto the Hollies' healing process. By about six weeks after my first healing session, the ends of live branches were filling out. Two more weeks—mid October—and the Hollies had abundant leaves.

I stepped into the Hollies' world. I allowed myself to listen at a deep place to their assessment of their condition and of what would solve their problems. It's the kind of thing you can do, too. Just try it!

TREE'S POINT OF VIEW: A MYSTERY SOLVED

Dr. Jim visits the countryside: A big old Catalpa was lagging behind others in leafing out during spring. It showed other signs of being stressed, including small leaves and dead branches. I used my Green Centrics™ System to get its inner parts and functions operating in harmony and in sync. At one point, I had to balance the whole tree's physiology to a foreign substance inside the tree. Over the years, the substance had caused the tree to weaken. The tree was continuously fighting it.

During the later steps of the process, the old tree told me—from its point of view—that the foreign substance was metal. I looked around the tree and did see old, rusty metal signs nailed into its trunk. But, the tree clearly indicated that the nails and signs were not the source of the metal problem. The metal came from another source.

I finished my treatment without knowing the source of the metal.

A few weeks later, I happened to be telling someone from a nearby town the story of the metal in that tree.

They said, "Oh! That tree is due east from where a coal-burning power plant is located."

I later asked the tree, and it confirmed that it accumulated an airborne source of metal in its structure—mystery solved! Just by looking at the tree, no one could know that accumulated metals were the cause of the weakness, unless they came from the tree's point of view.

Just by looking at an old tree, we might forget that it was once young and living under different circumstances. The Catalpa was younger when the coal-burning power plant was venting heavy metals into the air. The west winds carried the metal toward the tree. As the tree aged, it gradually took more and more of the metals inside of its physiology. After many years, the accumulated metals along with other additive environmental stress factors weakened the tree's inner physiology to the point where it showed stress and decline.

There is nothing that anybody can do to get metals out of a tree's tissues. However, my treatment can balance the tree's bioenergy to the presence of metal in its physiology. The tree did recover and lived to be a healthy tree.

TREE'S ROOTS' POINT OF VIEW: POT-BOUND TREES

Dr. Jim tells: My customer's home was on a hillside. The Beech tree she asked me to treat was looking stressed. I did my normal Green Centrics™ treatment. At one point, I had to balance the tree to where it lived. I quickly understood—coming from the root's point of view—that there was some constriction in the growth of the roots and that the roots could not grow any deeper.

As I explained this insight to the caretaker, she nodded in understanding. She said that not very far underneath the soil surface was a layer of shale rock. This would explain why the roots could not grow deeper. After treatment, I gave the caretaker some practical tips such as watering on the upside in the heat of summer. The Beech recovered.

Similarly, an Oak tree was growing between another customer's garage and the neighbor's house. Coming from the Oak's point of view, the roots were pot bound and the tree was showing signs of stress. When the tree was small, it thrived there. As it became larger, the space was too small. I told the tree it could send out roots in the direction of the neighbor's open yard. At the same time, I told the customer to warn the neighbor not to disrupt the yard because that would hurt the tree. The Oak fully recovered.

TREE'S BRANCH'S POINT OF VIEW: ROCKS ARE WEDGES

Basia relates: During a trip to meet a friend and graduate, this weathered old tree on the Airport Mesa, Sedona, Arizona, called out for help.

Sylvie and I were happy to assist it.

During our Tree Whispering® treatment, we saw that the tree's branches were separating from its trunk. Then we discovered the cause. It is a common practice in Sedona—a mecca for seekers and people wanting healing—to use the local red rocks to represent their own burdens. They put the rocks down in order to symbolically release their burdens. It is a prayerful process for most people.

Unfortunately, many people were using this tree and others as repositories for their burden-rocks. We found hundreds of long, narrow, red rocks wedged into spaces between branches and the trunk; we even found them inside holes in the trunk.

From the tree's branch's point of view, those rocks served as mechanical wedges to force apart growing tissue. Those rocks were killing the tree. It seemed to me a high price to pay for helping people release their burdens.

Trees—as Life Forms—are the most generous of Beings. This particular tree bore its own burden of rocks with serenity but told us through our intuitions that it was relieved when we removed the rocks and released the burdens that the rocks carried.

Insight 9:
Trees and Plants Tell the Truth

Dr. Jim tells the truth about people's lies: On many, many occasions when treating trees and plants on people's properties, I have had to balance the Green Being's natural functionality to the presence of some product that was applied to it.

See, trees and plants use precious resources to clear foreign substances out of their systems in much the same way that people's livers purify blood. In all cases, I ask property owners or managers what they put on the tree or plant. Sometimes the people are straightforward and tell me what was done.

Sometimes, I get an evasive answer: "Oh, nothing." I continue to ask until they admit that they used something-or-other on the tree or plant.

Green Beings tell the truth.

TELLING THE TRUTH: CHEEKY SOYBEANS

Dr. Jim says: Years ago, I was working with an organic soybean grower. In one field, the crop showed a thin stand, weak and unhealthy. After my third attempt to get the truth from him, I politely told him that I had to perform a balance between the soybeans and something that was applied to the field. He finally conceded that he used some kind of soil augmentation product bought from a catalog that sold primarily human-based health products. The soybeans told the truth!

TELLING THE TRUTH: WILLOWS WITH ALIEN DNA

There was a couple who asked me to check their stand of Willow trees at an old farm. They failed to tell me that the trees had been genetically modified. I started to work on the trees. I felt a sense of a dark presence in the area. Initially, I had to balance the trees to the presence of a foreign material inside them.

It was then that the phrase "genetically modified" came to me. So I asked the trees. They told me that they were fighting the foreign genes in their DNA. The trees knew they were changed and they didn't like it. *61*

I have a passionate distaste and loathing for the practice of genetic modification with trees and plants. It is putting an entirely alien force into the genetic structure, bioenergy, and the Life Force of a Green Being. The tree or plant is fighting the inappropriate DNA all of its life. The genetic modification compromises the individual's natural processes and inner functionality, and ultimately risks the entire species.

The Willows at the farm preferred to subsist on their own. They did not want me to bring them into a higher state of health. I left there very sad that humans would tinker with such arrogance and disrespect for Mother Nature's creations.

TELLING THE TRUTH: BAD DIGESTION FOR THIS HONEY LOCUST

Dr. Jim on another golf course: The assistant superintendent of a well-known golf course in the Northeast United States brought me in to do healing treatments on a few key trees. The president of the course, who can play golf on the days that the course is closed, asked what I was doing. The assistant explained. The golf course president understood and said, "Take a look at the tree in front of my house."

After I had my hands on the Thornless Honey Locust in front of his house, it was clear to me that something had been sprayed on it that did not agree with it.

I asked the assistant, "What was sprayed on the tree?"

He said, "Nothing. If anything had been applied to the tree, I would have been told about it."

I asked him to double-check. A few days later, he called with the news. Without his knowledge or approval, an outside contractor had applied an insecticide to the tree. Trees always tell the truth!

TELLING THE TRUTH: SOMETIMES ONLY THE TREE KNOWS

Dr. Jim smiles and recalls the scene: Sometimes people don't know what the truth is, but the trees do know.

In a coastal California town, an enormous and historic tree was mysteriously ailing. The past town arborist really loved this tree and asked me to help it. He told Basia and me that he cared for this tree so much he would check on it after a storm before he did anything else.

On the day Basia and I arrived, three arborists—including our host—and three contractors greeted us. We found the tree in a very small, triangular town park, bordered by a large highway, a small road, and a parking lot on the third side.

Everyone had their theory about what was going on with the tree. Some thought it was too close to the main highway and the problem was pollution. Others felt that carvings into the trunk were a problem. Still others blamed compaction of the soil. Someone even mentioned that homeless people liked to visit the tree and may have used it as a bathroom. These theories were all logical and sensible best guesses from their human point of view.

Then, I put my hands on the tree. I took on its point of view. The first thing I felt from the tree was the sensation that it wanted to move toward the main highway. In fact, I felt that if the tree could have stood up and walked over to the highway, it would have done it. That's how strong the feeling was. This phenomenon gave me a clue that perhaps the tree wanted to move away from something on the opposite side.

The parking lot was on the opposite side. My heart posed the question to the tree, "Is there something in the parking lot that is hurting you?" The tree replied, "Yes."

Through a series of questions, I found out that a problem happened in the parking lot about 80 years before, and was affecting the tree now.

I paused my treatment to talk to the group. I suggested, "If you tell me what happened in that parking lot about eighty years ago, I will tell you what is going on for that tree."

They put their heads together in conference while I went back to the tree to continue my healing treatment.

I repaired the internal functionality including circulation and photosynthesis. After the tree told me that healthy patterns were now reestablished, one additional problem came up. It said that its roots were being *stung* whenever heavy rains occurred. So, I gave some additional attention to the functionality of the roots to help strengthen them. This whole process took about an hour and a half.

I returned to the group to discover that they had solved the mystery. About eighty years before, the town experienced an earthquake. Much debris from the earthquake was dumped into the area that is now under that parking lot. This information completed the puzzle.

Dr. Jim continues: During that eighty-year period, the canopy of the tree grew much larger. Correspondingly, the roots extended their growth toward the parking lot. Now, when it rained, some of the run-off from any remaining debris was adversely affecting the tree. The tree had to continuously tolerate this stinging effect when it rained. Over time, the tree's inner operations were weakened.

My treatment repaired the tree's internal functionality. It also helped to strengthen the roots to resist the effects of the run-off.

As a practical solution, the contractors discussed the possibility of installing a dam in the earth between the parking lot and the tree's roots, thinking that might help.

In any case, the tree went on to be healthy and continued to grow. All along, the tree knew the truth of what was wrong.

All I had to do was come from the tree's point of view and ask it.

Insight 10:
Assumptions Put People Out of
Balance with Nature

Basia offers some views on balance: Have you ever stood on a rock with a rippling stream flowing all around you? Were you steady on your feet? Was the rock buried deep enough in the stream-bed to be steady or did it teeter-totter on another rock? Did you *almost* fall in—but saved yourself by stretching your arms, bending your legs, or shifting your torso?

Our ability to balance our bodies depends on inputs from our senses about body position while our muscles make fast adjustments. Stability results—or not. Maybe you shifted and swayed but fell in the stream anyway.

Dr. Jim and I will talk about what balance means in a larger context later, but, first, Dr. Jim tells two important stories about how trees physically balance themselves.

OUT OF BALANCE: OAK ON THE EDGE

Dr. Jim says: I worked on a seventy-five-year-old Oak that was living on the edge of a sheer twenty-foot cliff. During my treatment, the tree told me it was well-balanced on the edge. I noticed a dead limb on the tree that had grown in the opposite direction of the drop-off.

I asked the tree, "Should the dead limb be cut off?"

OAK LIVING ON EDGE OF CLIFF: Oh, no! Please don't cut off that limb. I use it to stay balanced on the cliff, especially in storms or high winds. Please allow me the chance to fill in and to grow new branches in the direction of the dead limb before you cut it off. This way, I can maintain my balance.

Dr. Jim continues: Trees understand balance. Living on the edge of a drop-off, this Oak was able to grow roots in only one direction, therefore natural limb placement and root growth had to compensate to create balance.

What about people who don't communicate with a tree; who don't ask it about pruning? They might see that dead limb and cut it off. We say that asking the tree allows the person to be in balance with Nature.

OUT OF BALANCE: OAK ON THE 18TH HOLE

Dr. Jim says: An Oak tree was a key feature on the 18th hole at a well-known golf course. It lived on the edge of a steep drop-off to a sandpit. I was called in because it was ailing. Before I arrived, someone removed a living limb that was opposite the drop-off. This limb was keeping the tree balanced. One of the early parts of my treatment was to work with the growth of the tree to set down more roots in the direction where the large limb was cut. This would help the tree balance itself and stop it from toppling over the drop-off on the opposite side. The Oak recovered its health after my treatment and it stayed upright.

Dr. Jim shifts the topic: Those stories have been about physical balance. But, what about enhancing dynamic balance among the Beings of Nature in whole ecosystems? When people come from a human point of view, the feelings and conclusions they have may *seem* correct because of humanity's long history of assuming that humans know best.

But there are mysteries in Nature. There are things people don't yet understand because they usually rely on only the left and logical brain. Using an open heart and the holistic perspective of the right brain, people can put themselves into personal balance.

Re-establishing dynamic balance in Nature—which is what Insight #10 is really about—begins with coming from a living Being's point of view, asking questions, and getting answers intuitively. I have been fortunate to receive many pieces of Nature's great puzzle, have been granted deep understandings, and have been given insights into some of trees' and plants' mysteries. I think that is because I have humbly and patiently put myself into their perspective—their point of view. You can too!

Basia continues with some views on balance: All of the creatures of Nature engage in their own unique balancing acts. They seek balance, not only as individuals maintaining upright stature but also as groups acting in ecosystems. The phrase "Balance of Nature" refers to the idea that ecosystems usually seek dynamic balance—called "stable equilibrium." In other words, predator species are linked to prey species (such as lions with antelopes) and herbivores are linked with their food sources (such as deer with foliage.) Such linked species need to live in balanced relationships so that both can continue to co-exist.

Continued survival and sustainably thriving seem to be critical and timely issues for each of us in our personal relationship with Earth as a whole as well as with the ecosystems that are close to home.

From Dr. Jim's and my standpoint as spokespersons for the Plant Kingdom and as guardians of the systems we teach, we suggest that many people rely on assumptions about Nature that result in (1) people being out of balance with Nature and (2) Nature going out of dynamic balance and into extreme fluctuations.

The essence of assumptions is that they are unquestioned. We ask you to question the truth of the following assumptions. We ask that you shift your attitudes and practices so that you can move to a higher level and broader perspective.

Assumption 1: Killing pests will solve a tree's or plant's problems.

Assumption 2: People can dominate and control the Plant Kingdom, the Insect Kingdom, and the world of microorganisms.

Assumption 3: Science and technologies have made people superior to Nature, therefore people don't have to ask other living Beings for input or wisdom in order to solve human problems.

Assumption 4: Humans play a win-lose game with the Beings of Nature.

Assumption 5: Each thing in Nature is independent. Impacting one does not impact others.

Dr. Jim elaborates on these often invisible assumptions: What about when a tree or plant has an insecticide, fungicide, or other chemical put on it? Let's talk about the assumptions that underlie the use of these kinds of products on trees and plants.

Generally, Assumption #1 says that people can control a pest by killing it, so that the tree's or plant's problems will be solved and it can grow again. False! Pests are not generally the cause of stress or decline in trees or plants. Weakness of inner physiology comes first, as we have already discussed.

Assumption #2 says that people can dominate the insect world and the world of microorganisms. Even when insects and microorganisms develop what is called "resistance" to products, people think that they can create stronger or better products to do the job of killing. The thinking that supports this assumption is flawed. Insects and microorganisms will always and ultimately evolve themselves in order to survive.

Dr. Jim suggests an enlightened choice: People can declare peace. People can learn to co-exist and cooperate with insects and microorganisms. All living Beings—including people—have their place and their purpose in Nature.

A shift in attitudes and consciousness is needed to wage *peace* and to *co-exist* with the rest of Nature. Co-existence means learning to live in dynamic balance with other life forms.

Dr. Jim reminds that all are connected: People have certainly heard about the web of life in Nature. There is an intellectual understanding that members of ecosystems are connected.

However, the way people act is often different.

In Assumption #5, I believe that people forget their connection to the web of life and assume that everything else is as separate as they may feel. So, some people are still spraying chemicals on their properties or killing members of their backyard ecosystems without regard to the larger impact.

When coming from the ecosystem's point of view, as I do, a deeper understanding is revealed: each member of the ecosystem is part of a bigger puzzle. By coming from the ecosystem's point of view, people can sense and deeply experience the total truth that impacting one member impacts all the members—*whether or not it can be seen or documented immediately.*

Basia highlights Assumptions #3 and #4: The third assumption is about arrogance; it's assuming that people know best and that science and technology make people superior. While it's true that the advances and conveniences that science and technology have brought do not have to be surrendered, the illusion of superiority which they give us needs to be examined.

Lastly, the way that concepts such as *survival of the fittest* were commonly interpreted led many people to view Nature as a grand competition requiring winners and losers. Now, assuming a fight, many people approach the Beings of Nature as if they are playing a win-lose, us-or-them kind of battle. That view often results in people killing living Beings that are perceived as harmful. People may win a few skirmishes to prevail over Beings of Nature seen as pests, but I say that humanity will ultimately lose that war.

Basia gives an example: I have uncovered lots of scientific research about efforts to make crops produce greater yields or to make plants more effective in repelling insects. As I read such scientific papers, I am struck by the scientists' assumptions underneath their good intentions.

If scientists assume that Nature can be controlled, dominated, and has no intelligence of its own, then those scientists may form and test hypotheses without considering the plant's point of view or long-term consequences. They may even go forward with their research without regard to far-reaching ramifications for the whole planet's delicate ecosystems.

For example: Genetic modification of living Beings seemed like a good idea to some people, and because they *could* do it, they *did*. No one knows how this grand experiment will turn out for humanity and for the whole planet. I say that such scientists are working in the vacuum of their own assumptions; they are out of balance within themselves and out of balance with Nature.

Basia suggests an alternative approach: However, imagine that the same scientists—or anyone, really—could shift their own consciousness by recognizing the intelligence in Nature, adopting attitudes of cooperation, partnership, and equality, and acting with enough humility to ask Nature—through perceptive abilities—for information and guidance about intended projects.

No longer would scientists—or anyone—be working in an entirely human-centric system. Instead, people *and* Nature's inherent consciousness would be equal partners in the quest to create a new form. The newly co-created form, project, or idea would *meet both human specifications as well as satisfy the wisdom, dynamic balance, sustainability, harmony, and vitality of Nature's Intelligence.*

In that way, human endeavors would be done consciously, respectfully, co-creatively, with wisdom, and in balance. The human desire for plants to become more productive could be done in a new, equal, and mutual partnership. The unworkable assumptions outlined above would be transformed.

Dr. Jim offers hope: You have learned about asking questions to trees, plants, and all of Nature's Beings so you already recognize them as partners. You know that they have valuable input. They can help us to solve our problems, both personal and environmental, *if asked.*

Dr. Jim describes how to make the shift: Invasive insects and invasive diseases are actually evidence of Nature being out of dynamic balance. While many people are striving to solve the problems of invasive organisms, most efforts end up supporting the problems. How can that be?

It is so because people are usually working inside of the same paradigm or mindset where the problems were created—beliefs and practices of domination, control, superiority, and separation.

Remember what Albert Einstein said? He said, "We cannot solve our problems with the same kind of thinking we used when we created those problems."

I suggest adopting a new set of consciously chosen beliefs and deliberate practices based on *partnership, cooperation, equality, and integration.* Taking those concepts to heart— along with the ideas live-and-let-live and we-are-all-connected— means shifting to earth-friendly, harmonious practices. And, that leads to a genuinely sustainable way of life. Basia and I think that such a relationship with Nature can result in the creation of an even higher quality of life than we currently enjoy.

Dr. Jim asks "what if?" What if people changed their attitude, "killing is the solution," to another attitude, "live and let live?" What if people changed their feeling that they are separate from other life-forms to "we are all connected?"

Dr. Jim paints a new picture: This shift would go beyond interacting with individual plants and go up to the scale of backyards or even larger bioregions. Here's how it could work.

Imagine people communicating intuitively with their trees as you have learned about in this book. Imagine people asking those plants what they need. Trees' and plants' answers might not be what people assume them to be.

Then, suppose people communicated nonverbally with the intelligence within insects and disease organisms? What if people asked them what they wanted? It might be a pleasant surprise. Suppose it was easier to work with them than people thought? Suppose they were willing to help us?

Suppose there could be some kind of compromise between two members of an ecosystem (such as the invasive organisms and trees) so that they could co-exist and mutually thrive?

Such an innovation is already here.

Forging such a compromise—like mediating an agreement—is possible. Basia and I call that kind of negotiation where *everybody wins* an EcoPeace Treaty™.

EcoPeace Treaties impact whole ecosystems. EcoPeace Treaties involve insects, diseases, and all other organisms—including people—coming into dynamic balance with trees and plants so that all can co-exist. Other books in this series and the website *EcoPeaceTreaties.org* expand on the concept and give examples of EcoPeace Treaties.[13] Live-and-Let-Live and we-are-all-connected are the fundamental principles behind Cooperative BioBalance®.

If people accept the new ideas and if they learn to use these technologies in partnership with all the Beings of Nature, then the goal of living and thriving in healthy, dynamically balanced, connected and interconnected, and sustainable ecosystems at backyard, local, and global scales is within reach—even in our lifetimes.

After all, all living Beings are connected. We can all co-exist.

It can be a live-and-let-live world.

Will you help create it and be a part of it?

With gratitude
   to you,
   to the Plant Kingdom,
   to all ecosystems and their members,
   to the fractal network patterns,
   and to all the living Beings of Nature.
Dr. Jim Conroy
Ms. Basia Alexander

Citations and More to Learn

1. Society for Plant Signaling and Behavior, mission statement on website, http://www.plantbehavior.org/about.html

2. Rollin McCraty, Mike Atkinson, Dana Tomasion, and William Tiller, "The Electricity of Touch: Detection and Measurement of Cardiac Energy Exchange Between People," K. H. Pribram, ed., *Brain and Values: Is a Biological Science of Values Possible?* (Mahwah, NJ: Lawrence Erlbaum Associates, Publishers, 1998): 359–379. Proceedings of the Fifth Appalachian Conference on Behavioral Neurodynamics.

3. Rollin McCraty, Raymond Trevor Bradley, and Dana Tomasino, "The Resonant Heart," *Shift: At the Frontiers of Consciousness*, December 2004–February 2005, p. 15. www.HeartMath.org/research/research-library/research-library.html#energetics-research

4. Beverly Rubik, PhD, "The Biofield Hypothesis: Its Biophysical Basis and Role in Medicine," *The Journal of Alternative and Complementary Medicine*, 8:6 (2002): 703–17. Published by Mary Ann Liebert, Inc., New Rochelle, NY. The article can be found at www.liebertpub.com/products/product.aspx?pid=26. The website is www.liebertonline.com. *Basia adds:* A colleague of Dr. Rubik's is Dr. Gary E. Schwartz, author of *The Energy Healing Experiments–Science Reveals Our Natural Power to Heal*. I recommend this book for a deeper understanding of bioenergy.

Basia adds: Take a look at the citations in our main book for more scientific references, *Tree Whispering: A Nature Lover's Guide to Touching, Healing, and Communicating with Trees, Plants, and All of Nature.*

5. www.cooperativebiobalance.org/about/technologies/

6. Edmund Bourne, *Global Shift–How a New Worldview is Transforming Humanity* (Oakland, CA: New Harbinger Publications, Inc., 2008), pp. 105–16.

7. Linda Walling, "The Myriad Plant Responses to Herbivores," *Journal of Plant Growth Regulation* 19 (2000): 195–216. http://www.cepceb.ucr.edu/resources/biblio.htm#phloem

8. J. Engelberth, H. T. Alborn, E. A. Schmelz, and J. H. Tumlinson, "Airborne Signals Prime Plants Against Insect Herbivore Attack," in *Proceedings of the National Academy of Sciences of the USA* 101:6 (2004): 178–85. www.ncbi.nlm.nih.gov/pmc/articles/PMC341853/

9. *Basia says:* No single reference will be sufficient to understand Quantum Physicists' views that everything—including you—is energy. Some physicists have taken the extra step to tie their studies to ancient spiritual views about oneness. You may want to start your journey of discovery at *WhatTheBleep.com*. Once, there, try going down that rabbit hole of non-linearity and paradox with *Down the Rabbit Hole,* a video.

10. www.TreeWhispering.com/Whispers

11. www.PlantKingdomCommunications.com/storeandmore/

12. http://en.wikipedia.org/wiki/Joyce_Kilmer

13. *The Tree Whisperer's 10 EcoSystem Insights, The Tree Whisperer's 10 Multi-Dimensional Insights.* See examples at *www.EcoPeaceTreaties.org*

© David Slade

The Institute for
Cooperative BioBalance®
Partnering with Nature
Balancing Invasives
Rejuvenating Eco-Systems

Together, Dr. Jim Conroy and Ms. Basia Alexander **co-founded** the Institute for Cooperative BioBalance®. **Its mission** is to

- *transform people's role from observers to protectors in their backyard, local, and global ecosystems,*
- *foster cooperative and equal partnerships among all of the Beings of Nature—including people,*
- *bring into people's daily lives the principles of Cooperative BioBalance (such as we-are-all-connected), Tree Whispering®, and bioenergy-based practices,*
- *make the dream of healthy, vigorously growing trees, plants, crops, forests, and ecosystems available to everyone, and*
- *revolutionize practices to follow a policy of live-and-let-live with invasive insects and disease organisms in ecosystems, bringing about sustainable dynamic balance.*

Jim Conroy, Ph.D., earned his doctorate in Plant Pathology from Purdue University and spent 25 years as a successful executive in top ag-chem companies. Now, calling himself The Tree Whisperer®, he is an author and visionary expert in Nature-based communication and a global authority who holistically heals trees, plants, and ecosystems with his own intuitive bioenergy-healing approach. His leading-edge professional system combines modern plant science with new sciences, ancient wisdom, and hands-on practices.

He achieves totally earth-friendly and truely sustainable results entirely without products, by healing compromised internal functionality. Reversing stress in trees, plants, forests, and crops, as well as establishing dynamic balance in ecosystems fragmented by invasive insects and diseases is his life's work. Because of his ag-chem background, he can relate to conventional approaches while bringing his innovations forward.

As creator of Tree Whispering, he teaches globally. In classes, people engage in healthy, inspiring, and profound connections with the living Beings of Nature. They can learn how to restore tree and plant health with easy, simple, heart-based "touch and focus" methods. Tree care professionals are invited to attend and expand their attitudes and practices.

He is a consultant to estates, forests, parks, and large gardens, a keynote speaker, certified organic landcare professional, and rose grower.   **DrJim@CooperativeBioBalance.org**

Ms. Basia Alexander is a catalyst for positive change. She is an author and innovative leader in the new—and paradigm altering—field of Conscious Co-Creativity. As an expert Nature communicator, she brings an experienced perspective and powerful techniques for advancing a new kind of relationship with the living Beings of Nature: partnership and cooperation as equal partners.

Basia co-leads Tree Whispering workshops and produces original curriculum including the new sciences and ancient wisdom underpinning this work. She leads a relaxing guided visualization experience that enhances people's ability to feel a deep—even spiritual—connection between themselves and living Beings of Nature.

As an Intuitive with Earth Elements, Basia writes on topics of creativity, transformation, and how to live in collaboration with the Beings and Spirits of Nature. Always on the leading edge, she created her own B.A. in Communications from Beloit College and is pursuing a Conscious Evolution Masters Degree at The Graduate Institute. She is also a coach, bioenergy healer, gourmet vegetarian cook, desktop publisher, and has lifelong experience as a container gardener.   **Basia@CooperativeBioBalance.org**

© Jane Kellner

The Institute for
Cooperative BioBalance®
Partnering with Nature
Balancing Invasives
Rejuvenating Eco-Systems

As **founders** of the Institute for Cooperative BioBalance, Dr. Jim Conroy and Ms. Basia Alexander believe that people's collaboration with Nature through Tree Whispering® and Cooperative BioBalance® promises the possibility of restoring livable dynamic balance within ecosystems and attaining sustainability—even in our lifetimes.

As **speakers and teachers**, they offer speaking engagements and lead **workshops**. Participants validate their deep connection with Nature and their core selves. They have "ah-ha" insights that lead them into better stewardship of their land. People magnify intuitive perception, improve well-being, and use easy, simple, heart-based "touch and focus" methods. They see trees—and their own world—through new eyes.

As **co-authors**, Dr. Jim and Basia inspire Nature lovers to adopt new ideas and practices. Their books champion do-it-yourself approaches, enlightened attitudes, educated environmentalism, visionary tree advocacy, and practical spirituality.

•Tree Whispering: *A Nature Lover's Guide to Touching, Healing, and Communicating with Trees, Plants, and All of Nature*
•Tree Whispering: *Trust the Path Notebook and Journal*
•The Tree Whisperer's 10 Tree and Plant Insights
•The Tree Whisperer's 10 EcoSystem Insights
•The Tree Whisperer's 10 Multi-Dimensional Insights
•People Saving their Trees in Hurricane Sandy: *TreeProtector.org*
•Messages From Trees: *A Coloring Book for the Young and Young-at-Heart*
•Stepping Inside the Plant's World: *Guided Visualization Exercises* (CD or MP3s)
•New Attitude About Nature Cards: *Set #1–Partnering with Nature*
•Words About Trees Inspirational Journal   •Words About Trees Poster

www.CooperativeBioBalance.org
www.TheTreeWhisperer.com
www.TreeWhispering.com
www.PlantKingdomCommunications.com

Tree Protector .org   **Are you a tree protector?** If you love trees or whole ecosystems, you are! Anything you do—from helping the trees in your backyard, to taking on city hall about trees in your town, to activism for healthy local and global ecosystems—makes you a tree protector!

TreeProtector.org
• serves people who love trees and ecosystems and who want to protect them from harm and degradation.
• tells the stories of Tree Protectors around the world—add your story!
• provides networking opportunities between Tree Protectors.
• offers supportive materials to people who want to holistically help the trees in their own backyards as well as protect trees in municipalities.
• offers inspiration to activists for local, regional, and global ecosystems.
• **TreeProtector.org/Kids** gives the young and young-at-heart a chance to share their messages from trees, to speak-up for trees, and more.